What Volunteers Should Know For Successful Fund Raising

Here, at last, is the complete and authoritative guide written specifically for volunteers who raise funds or are responsible for the financial health of gift-supported organizations. It is designed to meet the needs of these volunteers at all levels—from the solicitor who seeks a modest annual gift to the chairman of a multi-million dollar capital campaign, from a committee member to the chairman of the board.

Most of the nation's 45 million volunteers need such a guide, for almost all of the 690,000 American organizations they serve require increasingly greater funds to offset inflation, cutbacks in federal support, and reduced advantages of charitable giving of the Economic Recovery Tax Act of 1981.

This book tells you what you should know about your prospective donors, what motivates people to give, how you can gain the donor's interest, how to overcome timidity, what tactics are most effective, what to do when you don't know the answer to a donor's question, why donors make large gifts, how pledges can be increased, and more. It offers guidelines for a mail appeal and it shows you how you can move up to positions of responsibility and recognition, how you can structure your organization for more effective fund raising. The author also provides a useful overview of recent fund-raising developments, and predicts the trends likely to emerge in the 1980s.

Professional (paid) fund-raisers will also find this book must reading, since their success depends on their ability to help volunteers secure donations.

What Volunteers Should Know For Successful Fund Raising

Maurice G. Gurin

A SCARBOROUGH BOOK
STEIN AND DAY/*Publishers*/New York

FIRST SCARBOROUGH BOOKS EDITION 1982

What Volunteers Should Know for Successful Fund Raising was originally published in hardcover by STEIN AND DAY/*Publishers*. This paperback edition has been updated.

Copyright © 1982 by Maurice G. Gurin
All rights reserved
Designed by Louis A. Ditizio
Printed in the United States of America
STEIN AND DAY/*Publishers*/
Scarborough House
Briarcliff Manor, N.Y. 10510

Library of Congress Cataloging in Publication Data
Gurin, Maurice G
    What volunteers should know for successful fund raising.
    Includes index.
    1. Fund raising.   2. Volunteer workers in social service.
    I. Title.
HV41.G96   361.7   81-48508
ISBN 0-8128-6150-7

The "Letter to the Editor," of November 8, 1979, titled "Don't Mess With Our Country's Charities," by John W. Gardner, © 1979 by *The New York Times* Company. Reprinted by permission. Also reprinted by permission of John W. Gardner.

The author gratefully dedicates this book to the many volunteers who over the years have taught him, a professional fund raiser, so much about his calling.

Contents

Preface   9

1. What a Volunteer Solicitor Should Know About Annual Giving Campaigns   11

2. What a Volunteer Solicitor Should Know About Capital-Funds Campaigns   39

3. What a Volunteer Leader Should Know About Fund Raising in General   63

4. What a Volunteer Should Know About Recent Fund-Raising Trends   93

5. What a Volunteer Should Know About Likely Future Trends   111

Appendices

A.	Why Donors Make Large Gifts	121
B.	Guidelines for Mail Appeal	122
C.	Procedure for Making a Foundation Request	127
D.	The Private Sector and Urban Problems	129
E.	A Fair Practice Code	131
F.	Designations of Donor Recognition	132
G.	Planned Gifts in Capital Campaigns?	133
H.	Capital Campaign Timetable	136
I.	Gift Tables	138
J.	Don't Mess with Our Country's Charities	139
K.	Why a Consultant?	141

Index   145

Preface

Over 45 million Americans—or almost one in five—volunteer their services annually for more than 690,000 gift-supported organizations that flourish throughout the United States. And most of these volunteers engage in some form of fund raising.

This book was written for the volunteer (unpaid) fund raiser.

The New York Public Library, the largest privately supported public library in the country, listed on May 25, 1979, a total of 84 books on fund raising; and not one of them was addressed specifically and solely to the volunteer fund raiser. There was no dearth of books for the professional (paid) fund raiser.

As a fund-raising consultant over the past few decades, the author was continually called upon to answer the many questions that volunteers have about fund raising, and their perceptive questions have helped him develop more definitive answers than he had originally offered.

To the questions that concern volunteers, this book presents specific answers and—what is equally important—the fund-raising rationales that place the answers in perspective and testify to their validity.

It is not the thesis of this book that all volunteer fund raisers have to know all about fund raising—either for their own edification or for more effective service to the causes of their choice. Many of them may be content to know no more about fund raising than is necessary for them to carry out their specific assignments.

But the assignments of volunteers cover a broad gamut: they range from the task of soliciting a modest gift for the annual support of a charitable organization to the leadership of a multimillion-dollar capital campaign for a gift-supported institution.

The requirements for these assignments also vary greatly. For a solicitor seeking an annual gift, a bare acquaintance with fund raising could be adequate; for a capital campaign chairman, a comprehensive understanding of fund raising would be useful, if not essential.

The content of this book was designed so that volunteers need read only those sections which relate to their particular interests or the fund-raising activities in which they are engaged.

But all volunteers, however limited their fund-raising interest or involvement, could benefit from reading more extensively. This would certainly be true of volunteers in leadership roles, as they have a broader interest and a greater need to know more about fund raising.

While this book was not written for professional fund raisers, it may be of interest to them as well because their major concern is—or should be—to provide volunteers with the guidance and materials they need for the effective solicitation of funds.

In writing this book, the author has tried to be both clear and explicit. The need of volunteers engaged in fund raising is for information they can understand and use.

Americans have had a growing fascination with philanthropy—and with fund raising as its instrument—since Colonial times. It is the expression of our unique concern with the fate of our fellows, and of our desire "to look after our own"—particularly those whose hardship or suffering makes special claims on our generosity.

And generosity is not in short supply in our country. Americans contributed a record total of $47.74 billion to privately supported organizations in 1980, according to the American Association of Fund-Raising Counsel, Inc.

This record was not achieved by the contributions of major philanthropists alone. It was made possible mainly by gifts, many of them very modest indeed, from millions of Americans who participate in philanthropy to the extent of their means.

It is the author's intention that this book be both a guide and a salute to the many millions of Americans who give of their time and substance—and prevail upon even more millions to lend their financial support—to the voluntary organizations that contribute so importantly to the quality of American life.

> Maurice G. Gurin
> New York City

1

What a Volunteer Solicitor Should Know About

Annual Giving Campaigns

Why Your Volunteer Services Are Needed

There is probably not one gift-supported organization in the country today that has enough capable volunteers to raise the funds it needs annually. If you have the fund-raising ability, then, you can volunteer to serve practically any organization that appeals to you—and be assured of a warm welcome.

Your volunteer services are in such demand because never before has there been such a proliferation of philanthropic organizations and such a constantly rising level of financial support required to maintain them. Adding to this demand is the continuing loss of women volunteers, who are taking paid employment in increasing numbers.

If you are now raising funds for an organization, you must believe in the importance of its program. You and the organization are both fortunate: you, for being able to serve a worthy cause; your organization, for having the benefit of your services.

If you do not presently enjoy such a relationship, you may be interested in exploring the opportunities for serving worthwhile causes. In that event, you may not be aware of the extent of the choice that is available to you.

What a Volunteer Solicitor Should Know About

Which Organizations You Can Choose From

The nation's gift-supported organizations, in all their range and variety, are open to you. They include: hospitals; health agencies; welfare organizations; educational and scientific institutions; agencies serving the young, the aging, the handicapped, and the underprivileged; churches; libraries and museums; botanical gardens; and theater, opera, and ballet companies.

Organizations like these exist in virtually every fair-sized community. Country-wide, their number has been variously estimated. A total of 691,627 of them were classified by the Internal Revenue Service as 501(c)(3) organizations (those whose donors' gifts are tax deductible) as of June 1975.

The Commission on Private Philanthropy and Public Needs issued a report in 1975 that identified a core group of 409,214 traditional privately-supported organizations. They included 350,000 religious organizations, 37,000 human-service organizations, 6,000 museums, 5,500 private libraries, 4,600 privately supported secondary schools, 3,500 private hospitals, 1,514 private institutions of higher learning, and 1,100 symphony orchestras.

Which Cause You Should Select

With so many worthwhile causes to choose from, you are less than fair to yourself if you agree to serve one simply because its leaders show the good judgment of trying to enlist you. Make your own choice. Select a cause which seems to you to be important and urgent enough to merit your best efforts.

Specifically, it should be a cause which moves you sufficiently to feel justified (if not completely comfortable) in asking your friends, as well as strangers, to support it financially. It should be one to which you yourself would be inclined to contribute.

Such a cause could be heart disease or cancer, if you personally rate these health problems among the most deserving of support. It could be a cause which you might not consider the most important but

ANNUAL GIVING CAMPAIGNS

which, because it is being neglected or inadequately supported, would derive a special value from your services.

Since you are volunteering your services, you might as well get the most out of it personally. For instance, if the disadvantaged children of the inner city are a special concern of yours, volunteer to help raise funds for a local agency that serves them.

There is no reason why your volunteer services should not advance your own interests. Indeed, you can function most effectively and derive the greatest personal satisfaction by soliciting for a cause which you consider to be both important and interesting. Therefore, pick the cause that's right for you.

Why Annual Gifts Are Needed

If you are going to raise funds for the organization you decide to serve, you will want to know why it needs contributions. Your organization is probably no different from practically every other nonprofit organization which needs contributions for its annual maintenance or operating support because its other sources of income do not provide sufficient funds to meet its annual budget. And its budget increases annually because of rising costs, which continue to exceed income.

An organization therefore needs more money each year to provide the same services it furnished the previous year. But while it costs more each year just to stand still, many an organization adds further to its budget because it feels it must meet the demands made upon it for increases in its current services or for new services.

There are usually limits to reducing a budget by effecting economies, for eventually this process will seriously impair an organization's basic services. Therefore, whether for inflation alone or for inflation and increased services, the average philanthropic organization must seek increased annual contributions from those who approve its objectives.

How much an organization must raise in annual gifts depends upon the gap between its other income and its total budget. Other income

What a Volunteer Solicitor Should Know About

could include the return from the investment of endowment funds, earned income (from the sale of goods or services), and subvention from the city, state, or federal government.

How Your Organization Raises Annual Funds

As a volunteer who offers to serve as a solicitor, you will certainly be interested in knowing how your organization goes about the task of raising its annual funds and what role you will be expected to take in that endeavor.

If yours is the average organization, it probably has a group of volunteers serving as an annual giving committee. If its role is limited, the committee's efforts may amount to no more than a mail appeal to previous and prospective contributors and may not even include an advance solicitation of members of the governing board (who should feel obligated to contribute before all others are asked).

If you join such a committee, you would probably be asked to review lists of donors and prospects, suggest additional prospects from among your acquaintances, and indicate those whom you would be willing to solicit for contributions.

You would most likely be asked to write to your prospects, and could even be given a form letter to use and adapt to your own style. You would not be asked to call on your prospects if the committee has never undertaken this more effective approach and assumes you would not take the trouble to make in-person solicitations.

How You Can Strengthen the Committee

If you are asked to write to your prospects, you could raise eyebrows (and the effectiveness of the annual giving effort as well) by announcing that you intend to call upon your prospects in person. And you can be sure (particularly if you make your own gift first to set an example) that whatever contributions you get would be larger than they would have been if you had written letter appeals.

You could also strengthen the role of the committee by inquiring

ANNUAL GIVING CAMPAIGNS

whether the members of the board of your organization are asked to make annual contributions. (It is amazing how many annual giving efforts today do not solicit board members, who should be the ones most concerned with the financial support of their organizations.) And if the answer you get is that the board has never been solicited, you could suggest that a change in this policy is long overdue.

If you take these initiatives, you will certainly be shaking up the committee—or its method of operating—to some extent. As a result, you may be viewed with some concern at the outset; but do not be surprised if before long you are asked to assume a position of leadership.

How Fund-Raising Potential Is More Fully Realized

But your organization may have a broader approach to annual giving. It may solicit its board members and make in-person calls on individuals capable of large gifts, and write only to those who can give more modestly.

It may also seek grants from local foundations with an interest in the organization's program, and contributions from corporations likely to be receptive. If it belongs to the local United Way, your organization receives an annual allocation from the funds the United Way receives from corporations and their employees.

And, finally, the organization may request funds from the government, since federal, state, and city funds are available to local agencies for some aspects of their programs.

If your organization appeals to all of these sources of support, it truly conducts an annual giving campaign; and it comes closer than most organizations to realizing its full fund-raising potential.

How an Annual Giving Campaign Is Structured

An organization with a broad-scale annual giving campaign requires a volunteer structure to solicit the various sources of support.

What a Volunteer Solicitor Should Know About

This structure could consist of only one committee if it includes sufficient numbers of volunteers capable of planning and conducting the various fund-raising activities that should be undertaken during the year. These activities could include:
1. Solicitation of the board for advance gifts (which can usually best be made by several board members who are influential with the other members). The board should be urged to achieve 100-percent participation, to contribute first to set the example for all other prospective donors, and to give generously in proportion to their individual means. (The members should never be asked to give the same amount; such an approach is not equitable and always results in a smaller total contribution.)
2. Solicitation of special gift prospects—previous and prospective donors capable of substantial gifts—who should be solicited in person by committee members who know and could be effective with them. These prospects should include individuals and foundations, as well as corporations (unless the organization belongs to the local United Way). The committee should set the level of gifts it seeks from these prospects; the level usually varies from organization to organization and from community to community.
3. Solicitation of general gift prospects—for contributions below the level set for special gift prospects—which is usually made by mail appeal. It could also include door-to-door neighborhood solicitations and apartment house canvasses if these techniques are effective in your community and if the committee can organize the large corps of volunteers needed for these efforts.
4. Sponsorship of a benefit for additional support from annual donors and for first-time gifts from those who have never contributed to the organization. Special income-producing projects and promotions could also be undertaken. These activities also require the recruitment of large numbers of additional volunteers.
5. Solicitation of grants from appropriate agencies at all levels of government (city, state, and federal), which are usually assumed by a member of the organization's professional staff but could be effectively assisted by influential committee members.
6. Relations with the local United Way (if the organization is a

member), which is most often maintained by the professional director but which could benefit from the participation of committee members with standing in the community.

How You Would Be Assigned

If you would like to help with the special gift solicitation, you would probably be asked to solicit prospects whom you know. If you are acquainted with foundation trustees or directors, you could be helpful with approaches for foundation grants. If you know officials of corporations, you could be asked to participate in requests for corporate contributions. If you know an official of a government agency that has funds your organization could qualify for, you could be useful in seeking a grant from that agency.

If you are like most volunteers, however, the chances are slim that you would have contacts with these sources of support, and requests to them are usually handled by the organization's volunteer and professional leadership.

You would therefore be most useful for soliciting individual prospects. They would include the so-called family foundations, which, because they are small and are essentially conduits for the donors' charitable giving, are usually solicited as if they were individuals.

You will certainly raise more money for the organization if you choose prospects whom you know than if you are arbitrarily assigned prospects whom you do not know. As a volunteer, you can insist upon accepting only those prospects whom you feel you would be comfortable and effective in soliciting.

Why You Have To Give First—To Get Gifts

You may not be told a basic principle of fund raising at the outset (probably out of a sense of delicacy), but you should recognize it: you can be most effective in soliciting the gifts of others by first making your own gift.

While you lend a measure of endorsement to a cause by contributing your services as a solicitor, nothing is more persuasive with

What a Volunteer Solicitor Should Know About

prospective donors than the example you set. Your own gift not only attracts other gifts; it also helps to set the level of gifts you seek. And it shows that you really believe what you tell your prospects: that your cause deserves generous support.

Your prospects have an interest in knowing—if not a right to know—what you, an advocate of the cause, have contributed. It is therefore appropriate, as well as important, to tell them what you have given.

This should not be embarrassing for you (if you have given generously in proportion to your means) or for them (since they are being asked to consider the same giving standard you have observed).

What Help and Guidance You Should Expect

As a member of the special gifts committee seeking gifts from individual prospects, you may be better informed generally than your organization on the prospects you know and have agreed to solicit, but you may not be in possession of all the pertinent information that could guide you in soliciting them (such as their particular philanthropic interests and their giving records to the organization). It is the organization's responsibility to provide this background information, which could assist you and the committee in evaluating your prospects' giving potential.

You should be briefed on the dollar goal of the annual giving campaign, the portion of the goal that the special gifts committee expects to raise, any strategies the committee may have devised to achieve its objective, its timetable, the types of recognition offered donors, and any campaign materials you could use.

These materials could include a printed folder and a return-addressed envelope for prospects, a list of the various ways a donor can give and their tax advantages, a sample appeal letter for use in writing prospects you cannot see, and the organization's most recent annual report. It could also include a list of gift opportunities and recognition categories (explained on pages 21-22 and 47-48). Such materials usually comprise a volunteer solicitor's kit.

You should be familiarized with the case—or the reasons the organization cites—for justifying its appeal for support. These rea-

ANNUAL GIVING CAMPAIGNS

sons, ordinarily detailed in a case statement, usually focus on the organization's need to maintain or expand its services. The strength of its case is the extent to which its services are currently relevant, urgently needed, effectively provided, and economically administered.

You should also be informed of any fund-raising policies of the organization which you should observe in your solicitation activities (such as whether only checks should be accepted for gifts of money, or what procedure to follow with gifts of securities).

If your organization currently is also conducting a capital-funds campaign, you should be told whether it accords number one priority to annual giving (because it will always be essential for annual operations) and therefore urges that donors' gifts of capital be over and above what they contribute to annual giving.

With this orientation, you should be able to answer any pertinent questions your prospects may ask about the organization or its services, and to make a persuasive case for their generous support of the campaign.

Why You Should Know More About Annual Giving

You may think you know enough now to get by as a solicitor, but you could function more effectively if you knew more about the annual giving campaign, so that you can more clearly understand it in its entirety and how you fit into the total scheme.

You should therefore find the rest of this chapter not only of general interest but also of specific value in terms of deepening your knowledge of fund-raising procedures, of related information that can be helpful, of insights into donor motivations and solicitation strategies, and of special types of fund-raising activities (such as benefits, telethons, and phonathons) which might have an appeal for you.

How the Campaign Goal Is Determined

The dollar amount of the annual giving campaign goal of your organization should be at least the difference between its expected

What a Volunteer Solicitor Should Know About

income from all other sources and its total budget—provided that such an amount would not be so unrealistic an expectation that it would discourage prospective donors in believing in its attainment.

Setting the goal requires a delicate balance between what is feasible and what is challenging. Prospects must believe that a goal can be achieved or they may not contribute at all; but they should also be challenged to give at their best—or at least better than they would give ordinarily.

Therefore, if the feasible amount that could be raised is less than the full amount needed to meet the annual budget, the goal could be increased to a reasonable extent beyond the feasible amount. The enlarged amount would represent a "stretch" goal; it would help raise the giving sights of donors and more closely approximate the actual need.

How the Campaign Timetable Is Set

In setting the timetable for its annual giving campaign, your organization probably bears in mind two basic considerations: when it needs funds during the year, and when its donors traditionally make their gifts.

Ordinarily, donors are solicited annually on the anniversaries of the dates on which they made their first gifts. This practice, which is not as efficient as soliciting them all at the same time, is based on the belief that donors prefer to give at those particular times. Occasionally, therefore, donor lists are screened to determine, if possible, which donors can be asked to renew their gifts at the same time and which ones can be most effectively solicited only on their anniversary dates. Prospective donors, since they have never given, are solicited at any time an organization thinks is most propitious.

How Prospects Are Scheduled for Solicitation

Unless your organization makes only a mail appeal to all its prospects simultaneously, it should set the order in which its prospects are

ANNUAL GIVING CAMPAIGNS

to be solicited. Campaign strategy usually calls for soliciting prospects "from the top down"—that is, starting with those who can give the most and ending with those who can give the least.

An organization with a fully developed campaign plan and structure should follow this sequence of solicitation: first, of the members of its governing board; then, of the special gift prospects; and, finally, of the general gift (all other) prospects.

The campaign timetable should reflect that sequence of solicitation. Assuming that your organization operates on a calendar-year basis, it should set the board solicitation early in the year and complete it before scheduling the special gift solicitation. And both these efforts should be concluded before the public announcement of the campaign, which should signal the start of the campaign's general (or public) phase, when all other prospects are solicited.

If the board members and special gift prospects are to be solicited in person, the timetable must allow for this more lengthy procedure. It must allocate adequate time for several of the most influential board members to solicit the other board members. It must provide even more time for special gift solicitors to be organized, to review and evaluate the giving potential of special gift prospects, to select those they will solicit, and to complete their solicitation assignments.

The solicitation of the general gift prospects that is undertaken by mail appeal should allow time for making about three mailings, as follow-up mailings have been found to produce many responses not previously elicited. The initial mailing and two follow-up mailings could be spread over four or more months.

How Gift Levels Are Suggested to Donors

Your organization may have two devices by which its solicitors can indicate in a relatively painless way the level of gifts they hope prospective donors would consider.

One device is to establish recognition categories for gifts at various levels; they could be (to give an arbitrary example): benefactor, $1,000 or more; patron, $500 or more; and sponsor, $100 or more.

Thus, prospects could be asked to consider being patrons, which many volunteer solicitors feel is less painful than asking them outright for $500. The prospects are often shown the listing of patrons in the annual report, which is the customary method of according donors public recognition.

Another device is to suggest to prospects gift opportunities at levels it is hoped they would consider. Here, as examples, are gift opportunities offered by two organizations:
1. $56 pays for eight hours of licensed practical nursing care for a cancer patient (Cancer Care)
2. $100 covers a student's laboratory fees for a year (United Negro College Fund)

Using this device, prospects can be asked whether they would consider a gift that would make it possible for a child from the city's ghettos to enjoy two weeks in the country. If the prospects indicate they want to give less, they can be asked to cover the cost of one week at camp, or to consider a more modest gift opportunity (an organization should have a number of opportunities at different gift levels).

Prospective donors generally do not like to be told that they have to give or what they have to give, but many of them appreciate knowing what an organization hopes they would consider giving. Gift opportunities and recognition categories are effective and acceptable ways of indicating the levels of gifts that are desired.

Recognition categories also enable organizations to upgrade donors' gifts, for they can be used to encourage donors in a low category to increase their gifts to qualify for a higher category.

You should be advised of your organization's recognition categories and its gift opportunities, for they could prove useful to you in soliciting prospects. And in the event that your organization has not established these devices, you could render it an important service by urging that it do so at the earliest possible date.

How Solicitation Methods Vary

Previously, two types of solicitation were mentioned: in-person and mail appeal. There are variations, however, and some of them may be used by your organization. It could therefore be useful to know

ANNUAL GIVING CAMPAIGNS

something about them. Here, listed in the order of their fund-raising effectiveness, are the most common ways of soliciting contributions from prospective donors:
1. The solicitor talks to the prospect in person.
2. The solicitor talks to the prospect over the telephone.
3. The solicitor writes to the prospect in longhand.
4. The solicitor writes a typewritten letter to the prospect.
5. The solicitor sends a mechanically reproduced letter, but with the prospect's name and address filled in.
6. The solicitor sends a mechanically reproduced letter to the prospect, but addressed only to "Dear Friend."

This list can be extended to include probably the worst kind of solicitation: the mail appeal that includes unordered merchandise, which is obviously used to make the recipient feel obligated to contribute (and which, incidentally, the recipient has no legal obligation to return).

The order of effectiveness, as illustrated by this list, reflects a basic tenet in fund raising: the more personal the approach, the more effective it is likely to be. It is much easier for a prospect to throw a mail appeal in the wastebasket (particularly if it is addressed to "Dear Friend") than to turn down a request from someone who has taken the trouble of appealing in person.

Why In-Person Solicitation Is Best

You may think that you have read enough about in-person solicitation already. Yet its importance cannot be overemphasized when, even in these times of fund-raising sophistication, many volunteers still think they can serve a cause effectively simply by signing their names to written appeals.

The many worthwhile causes now seeking support have made the competition for the philanthropic dollar keener than ever before. In this competition, only the in-person solicitation has a good chance for the substantial contribution.

The mail appeal can be justified for those prospects whose giving potential may not warrant personal calls or for whom solicitors are

23

What a Volunteer Solicitor Should Know About

not available. Even in these circumstances, however, the mail appeal should be personalized to the greatest possible degree.

When In-Person Calls Cannot Be Made

You will find that there will be times an in-person call on a prospect will not be possible. A personal phone call would then be the next best alternative available to you; and it could be strengthened if it were followed by a personal letter that restates and develops further the case for support you made over the phone.

Finally, when you can neither see nor phone a prospect, you will have to resort to an appeal by mail. If your organization's campaign material includes a sample appeal letter that contains the basic elements of the case for support, adapt and personalize it so that it sounds like it is coming from you (or it will carry no conviction) and is meant for the specific prospect you are addressing (or it will read as though it is intended for anybody and therefore for nobody in particular).

Personalize the letter further by writing it on your own stationery; and use longhand if you write legibly—otherwise have the letter typed, so you don't put your prospect to needless effort. And enclose any material you think would be helpful, including a return envelope addressed to the organization (for the prospect's contribution).

How To Gain the Prospect's Interest

Arranging for a meeting should present no problem if you have agreed to solicit only prospects you know. Start by describing the essential services your organization provides, which is why you personally support it and seek the support of others. Explain how these services advance a cause which is important both to you and your prospect.

Suppose, for example, that your organization serves disadvantaged youth. Learn whether it is doing more than meeting some of their physical needs, whether it is also helping alienated youngsters feel that

ANNUAL GIVING CAMPAIGNS

they too have a stake in the community's well-being and is therefore helping them grow into responsible citizens.

If indeed this is the effect of its services, then the larger mission of your organization is to help keep the city viable. And your prospect has—or should have—a personal interest in the success of this mission, since it is also working in his behalf and therefore deserving of his support.

When To Ask for a Gift

Once you have gained the prospect's interest in your organization, you can start to talk about the funds it needs for the current year's operations and the importance of the prospect's contribution to the success of the fund-raising effort.

Make sure, however, that you do not inadvertently give your prospect the impression that your organization is in financial difficulties in general. The fact that your organization needs annual support—which practically every organization requires—should not even imply that it is not in a healthy financial condition. This is an important distinction, for donors usually do not prefer to contribute to financially unstable or ineffectively managed organizations.

When you think it is time to speak to your prospect about a gift, don't hesitate to indicate the extent of your own commitment—in terms of time, as well as money—for your example can be effective persuasion.

How To Help Your Prospect Decide on His Gift

Before your prospects volunteer an amount, indicate to them what you hope they will consider giving. It could be a gift opportunity or a recognition category (such as those listed on pages 21, 22, 47, 78, and 132. It is sound fund-raising strategy to select gift opportunities or recognition categories at levels at least a little higher than you think your prospects would ordinarily choose. In this way, you could raise their giving sights.

If your prospects are not inclined to decide on what to contribute at the outset, your own judgment should guide you on whether to press for a decision or ask them to think about it.

Should your prospects decide at once and give less than you hoped for, you ordinarily have no alternative than to thank them for their gifts. Subsequently, if you keep them informed of the effective use that the organization is making of gifts like theirs, the chances are they will renew—and possibly increase—their gifts the following year.

If your prospects are undecided and you ask them to think about what they may want to give, leave with them a folder on the organization, an annual report, and a return addressed envelope. Write to them the next day to thank them for their consideration of a gift, and restate briefly the case for support that you made to them in person. And if, after a decent interval, they do not send gifts, follow up with a phone call to them.

What Follows the Solicitation Call

Report promptly to your organization on the result or progress of your solicitation. Your organization may have a solicitor's assignment form on which it has listed the prospects assigned to you; it provides space for you to note the progress you have made and the final results you have achieved. If you have this form, use it to keep your organization posted on your activity; otherwise, report by letter or telephone.

Your organization has undoubtedly established an acknowledgment procedure for the receipt of annual gifts, and you should be familiar with it. It probably calls for the treasurer to send donors an official receipt form (for use with their federal income tax return) and for the campaign chairman to write them letters of appreciation.

As the solicitor, you would want to write your own thank-you letters to prospects who make gifts. It would also be advisable for you to make sure that your organization receives any gifts that your prospects promise to send, that they are appropriately acknowledged, and that the donors are given every recognition for which their gifts qualify.

ANNUAL GIVING CAMPAIGNS

How To Deal with Tax Deductibility

You should not stress the tax deductibility of annual gifts. Most prospects make relatively modest annual gifts and would therefore have little reason to be concerned with tax deductions; prospects capable of substantial contributions are usually well informed by their tax advisers on the tax advantages of any gifts they choose to make.

Since prospective donors can take tax deductions on gifts to any number of nonprofit organizations, your organization holds no special appeal for them in this respect. Your appeal must focus on what gifts to your organization would mean in terms of the services they could provide and the satisfaction the donors would derive from helping to make those services possible.

It is therefore advisable to mention only at the end of your solicitation that contributions to your organization are tax deductible to the full extent provided by law. Your campaign material should indicate the ceiling on tax deductibility for your organization, and the tax advantages of the various ways a donor can contribute (such as by cash or securities).

If prospects raise questions which your campaign material does not cover, tell them you will check with the appropriate organization official or, if they prefer, you will arrange for them to meet with that official (who could be a member of the professional staff, a volunteer leader, or an outside consultant to the organization).

What You Should Know About Fund-Raising Costs

You may get an occasional question from prospects about the cost of fund raising to your organization, and you should therefore be informed on the percentage of the total funds it raises that are attributable to fund-raising expenses.

This information should be included in the orientation your organization provides for volunteer solicitors, as well as in its annual report. Equally important is your organization's rationale for its fund-raising costs, since the conditions under which it raises funds differ at least in some respects from those of other organizations.

What a Volunteer Solicitor Should Know About

Fund-raising costs of organizations vary greatly. According to the National Information Bureau, which monitors such costs and sets standards of "reasonable expenses," the range can be as broad as from 3 percent to 70 percent. The Bureau's rule of thumb is that costs of 30 percent or more "raise questions" and that costs that approach 40 percent are not reasonable.

The Bureau's statistics on fund-raising costs of national voluntary health organizations show that these costs range from one percent to 41 percent, with most organizations' costs somewhere in the middle.

Some state governments now include in their regulations affecting fund-raising activities a provision that sets an arbitrary ceiling on fund-raising costs; your organization should know whether such a ceiling has been set in your state. Many charitable organizations would consider any arbitrary limitation as manifestly unfair.

If a prospect asks you fund-raising questions you are not prepared for, promise to obtain the answers and seek the information from the chairman of your campaign committee or a staff member of the organization's development department.

When To Break or Bend the Rules

The rules in soliciting are methods based on fund-raising experience that are considered to be generally applicable. But there are occasions, you will find, when they may not apply. Then, of course, they should be broken—or at least bent—to meet the needs of the particular circumstances.

Obviously, prospects do not always submit to the most effective means by which they can be solicited. Their refusal to be solicited in person could be due to a variety of reasons, including: (1) they do not want to be in a position in which they think they could be pressured into giving generously or giving at all, (2) they feel they would be embarrassed if they intend to give little or nothing, and (3) they would simply prefer to be dealt with at a distance.

Whatever the reason, a prospect's refusal to be seen has to be respected. The same is true if a prospect insists on being solicited by

ANNUAL GIVING CAMPAIGNS

mail. But when you encounter only mild resistance, you should feel an obligation to try to arrange for a personal visit.

Many organizations, which have traditionally conducted their annual giving campaigns solely by mail appeal, resist—or find it difficult to initiate—personal solicitation of their largest donors even when their financial needs can no longer be expected to be met by mail appeal.

Of course, a case could be made that almost all prospects would prefer not to be solicited in person and would much rather receive a mail appeal, which (if they were unreceptive) could be declined with far less embarrassment. But that is the very reason why in-person solicitations are preferred: they make it more difficult for prospects to decline or to make token contributions.

What To Do When You Don't Know the Answer

No matter how much you learn about your organization, sooner or later a prospect will ask you a question you are unprepared for. When this occurs, there is no substitute for honesty. Admit that you don't have the answer, but promise to get it.

And if the question is a particularly perceptive one, it will be flattering to the prospect if you tell him that—to your knowledge—he was the first to ask it. Such a prospect can often develop a special interest in your organization—particularly if you get him the information he requested, and thank him for his interest and for adding to your knowledge of the organization.

In a situation where you cannot put off an immediate answer to a question you are not prepared for, you have no choice but to use your best judgment in formulating one; it should be based on your knowledge of the character of your organization and its general policies, as well as your own notions of good sense and good taste. And then add that you will check with the organization to confirm your answer.

You have no reason to be concerned by an occasional question that poses a problem for you, assuming that you are well informed generally on your organization. Indeed, such occasions can provide part of the challenge of your assignments.

What a Volunteer Solicitor Should Know About

Even a professional fund raiser, who should know the answers, should not be right 100 percent of the time. Who likes anyone who is perfect? And besides, who can be correct all the time in fund raising, which is certainly not an exact science.

How Timidity Can Be Overcome

If you are timid, you should recognize that you are like most people when they first ask for contributions to charitable organizations. Relatively few people are free of timidity and feel completely comfortable at the outset.

One way to overcome timidity, of course, is by practice. The more solicitation calls you make, the more effective you become and the less uncomfortable you feel. And the gratification that comes from a successful solicitation (there are few satisfactions more rewarding than obtaining a big gift for your organization) should tend to make you view the next solicitation as more of a challenging opportunity than an intimidating problem.

Another way is to keep in mind that you are not asking for yourself. If you are like most volunteers, you would probably starve before asking anyone for 50 cents for your own use. But many such volunteers have come to recognize the great difference it makes when they ask for gifts for a cause in which they believe and personally support—for they are not asking for anything for themselves and they are not seeking from others anything that they themselves have not given.

A further way is to appreciate other people's good instincts and their potential generosity, which your solicitation could release. Many prospects have been grateful for the opportunity to contribute to good causes; and your prospects could also be appreciative, once they recognize the value and importance of your organization's program—to themselves, as well as to those it serves directly.

It would be useless to try to improve on the eloquent statement made in 1933 by John D. Rockefeller, Jr., whose massive philanthropies (totaling $552 million) certainly qualified him to express the perceptive feelings of a prospective donor:

ANNUAL GIVING CAMPAIGNS

When a solicitor comes to you and lays on your heart the responsibility that rests so heavily on his; when his earnestness gives convincing evidence of how seriously interested he is; when he makes it clear that he knows you are no less anxious to do your duty in the matter than he is, that you are just as conscientious, that he feels sure all you need is to realize the importance of the enterprise and the urgency of the need in order to lead you to do your full share in meeting it—he has made you his friend and has brought you to think of giving not as a duty but as a privilege.

Never think you need to apologize for asking someone to give to a worthy object, any more than as though you were giving him an opportunity to participate in a high-grade investment. The duty of giving is as much his as is the duty of asking yours.

Mr. Rockefeller was probably solicited for as many causes as anyone who ever lived; his reactions as a prospective donor should therefore lend encouragement and reassurance to any volunteer soliciting for a good cause.

How Publicity Can Be Useful

Publicity can provide a favorable environment for fund raising, but it can never substitute for the solicitation of prospects. Here are two examples:

Even front-page newspaper coverage of a major disaster in a foreign country does not relieve CARE, the voluntary agency for aid and development overseas, from appealing directly to its contributors if it wants the funds to respond to that emergency situation.

The Fresh Air Fund, which provides free summer vacations in the country for disadvantaged children in New York City, certainly benefits from the invaluable promotion it receives in the New York *Times,* and the total of the donations attributable to this promotion is considerable. But the Fund must still seek the major portion of its annual giving goal directly from its contributors.

A gift-supported organization ordinarily tries to gain publicity in the press, radio, and television just prior to the start of its annual

What a Volunteer Solicitor Should Know About

giving campaign; thus, there is a better chance that its prospects will recall the organization and its services when they are solicited for contributions.

Some organizations recognize that such publicity alone is not enough, and that they need to keep their good works continually (or at least periodically) in the public eye. As part of their year-long publicity program, they use the annual report as the basis of a press release and they plan special events designed to create favorable publicity.

Your organization can be expected to advise you of any publicity or promotional activity it plans that will coincide with the solicitation assignments it has asked you to undertake.

How Benefits Help Annual Giving

Many organizations raise a part of their annual giving goals by sponsoring one or more benefits during the year. As a member of the annual giving campaign organization, you could be asked to help sell tickets to a benefit.

Those who attend a benefit pay more than the cost of holding the event; the "profit" that is realized is a contribution and is applied toward the annual giving campaign goal.

Benefits vary with the tastes and the capacity of the individual organization. One organization holds a theater benefit; another stages a garden party; still another conducts an antiques auction.

Benefits are productive for fund-raising purposes if they elicit additional contributions from regular donors and first-time gifts from prospects who have never before given. If they meet this requirement, they supplement the funds which organizations raise through their other annual giving campaign activities.

Benefits can have other values. If well conceived and effectively promoted, they can attract favorable publicity for organizations and further public understanding of their services. They can also provide useful involvement of volunteers who like to participate in such undertakings.

ANNUAL GIVING CAMPAIGNS

What Projects and Promotions Include

Organizations raise annual funds through projects and promotions, as well as benefits. It could be useful to note how projects and promotions differ from special events and what they include.

Projects could be publications, such as a journal, for which paid advertisements could be solicited from local merchants and complimentary greetings from an organization's members and friends.

Other projects could be a bazaar with booths featuring different types of merchandise for sale, auctions for the sale of items donated by an organization's members and local merchants, and a thrift shop which can operate the year round.

Such income-producing projects should be carefully planned, as they can represent a substantial commitment by an organization in terms of both funds and volunteer service.

Promotions could include a wide variety of items or services that an organization can promote for profit. Among the items it could promote are personalized stationery and cards for the major holidays, which an organization can sell to its members and, through them, to their friends.

It can also produce for sale its own calendar, which could include important programs scheduled for the year, dates of other interesting events, and birthday and wedding anniversary dates of members, as well as commercial and complimentary advertisements.

An organization can promote any of its activities that have popular appeal. A summer camp for children, if it sponsors one, could have such appeal.

How Telethons and Phonathons Depend on Volunteers

Telethons and phonathons are conducted by organizations and institutions usually to raise annual funds, and both are dependent upon the services of volunteers on a once-a-year basis.

Volunteers who are too shy to solicit prospective donors either face-to-face or indirectly by mail can serve one of the growing number

What a Volunteer Solicitor Should Know About

of organizations that need volunteers to man the telephones and record the pledges that are phoned in by viewers. The telethon itself "solicits" the viewers, so no solicitation is required of the volunteer on the phone.

Many volunteers find this service interesting and rewarding because of the importance of the cause, the camaraderie of working with other volunteers in a group, and the attraction of television (which often shows them taking pledges on the battery of telephones that is set up for a telethon).

Telethons are conducted annually by health agencies on a local, regional, and national basis; and by hospitals on a local and regional basis. Both types of organizations recruit telephonists from among their regular volunteer workers.

Volunteers who want to participate in phonathons cannot be shy about soliciting over the telephone, for that would be their specific assignment. Indeed, they should have an effective telephone technique.

Phonathons usually are conducted annually by community hospitals and alumni associations of privately supported colleges. In each case, the organization arranges with the telephone company to install in an appropriate facility a battery of telephones to be used by volunteer solicitors on one or more occasions, usually at night when prospective donors are most likely to be at home.

The phonathons for both types of organizations are usually regional in scope. Hospitals recruit telephonists from among their regular volunteers; alumni associations enlist participants from the alumni body and preferably from the same class as the prospective donors they will be asked to solicit.

The appeal for both types of organizations is usually in behalf of the annual giving campaign; the prospects are mainly previous donors; and the case is the need for greater funds. Prospects are therefore asked to renew and, if at all possible, increase their annual giving.

What Motivates Prospects To Give

You don't have to hold an advanced degree in psychology to be an

ANNUAL GIVING CAMPAIGNS

effective solicitor; indeed, it probably could be argued that it is far better if you don't. That is because people generally do not like to have their motivations explored or to be manipulated in any way.

Much, of course, has been written about the motivations behind philanthropy; they range from a desire to expiate guilt or gain public recognition to an expression of unselfish concern or an awareness of a common humanity (see Appendix A).

This can be heady stuff—and of more danger than value. The safest and most effective approach for a solicitor is to attribute to a prospect what he would like to have attributed to himself. There can be no loss—and sometimes surprising gain—in assuming that the prospect is generous; and that if he understands the value of the cause you espouse, he will respond favorably.

Fund-raising experience seems to indicate that people give to organizations which provide worthwhile services and are led by leaders they respect. They usually give most generously to organizations with which they are actively involved, or which have special or important use for their gifts.

It is doubtful whether, for practical purposes, this fascinating and precarious subject need be explored further.

What You Can Do Most Effectively

You can be most effective as a solicitor because you are volunteering your time and effort to a cause, and seek to gain nothing financially from the success of your solicitations. Prospective donors cannot suspect you of having a selfish interest in the cause or of benefiting personally from any contribution they may make.

Your position is unassailable: you are working as a volunteer in behalf of a cause because you believe it is in the public interest and its successful advancement will serve the general good; and it is in that spirit that you seek to persuade others who, if they understand the reasons for your advocacy, could lend their support.

A professional fund raiser cannot assume this position with a prospective donor, simply because he is paid for his services.

As a volunteer solicitor, you possess another advantage. Your

What a Volunteer Solicitor Should Know About

contribution and status in the community is probably equal to, if not above, the level of gift you seek and the standing of the prospective donors you solicit.

But even a volunteer whose financial resources are less than those of his prospects can successfully solicit them if he gives as generously (in proportion to his means) as he asks them to give, and if they recognize him as a respected advocate of the cause he represents.

There are, however, occasions when a professional is called upon to take a direct role with sources of support. A member of the professional staff of a large foundation may want to deal with a professional staff member of a gift-supported organization, but it is usually just to obtain additional information in connection with a request it has received for a grant. For the same purpose, a member of a corporation's contributions committee may want to relate to a privately supported organization on a professional level.

Some organizations employ paid solicitors because they cannot enlist volunteers or do not want to accommodate to volunteers' part-time availability. This practice is not viewed approvingly by the overwhelming majority of the nation's gift-supported organizations.

How Volunteers and Professionals Differ

Volunteers contribute their time and energies to raise funds for a charitable organization. They serve when their time permits, since they have other calls upon their time—such as earning a living or running a household.

Their knowledge of fund raising varies greatly: some volunteers may be almost totally uninformed; others may be as informed as many professional fund raisers. Their ability at fund raising is just as varied; some may have difficulty asking for a modest annual gift; others may be fully capable of providing volunteer leadership for an annual giving campaign.

Professional fund raisers, because they are paid for their services, can be expected to be on duty throughout the entire working day. The abilities and experiences of professionals also vary: some are only qualified as specialists in a specific area of fund raising (such as

ANNUAL GIVING CAMPAIGNS

seeking foundation grants), while others have the ability and experience to furnish overall planning and direction of an annual giving campaign.

Volunteers and professionals contribute in different ways to campaign policy and prospect solicitation. Professionals advise on campaign policy matters; volunteer leaders make the campaign policy decisions. Professionals provide guidance and materials for solicitation assignments; volunteer workers call upon prospects for their contributions.

The success of an organization's fund raising depends in large part on an effective partnership of volunteers and professionals, and that partnership is never more effective then when it is based on a clear recognition by each partner of the value of the other's services.

2

What a Volunteer Solicitor Should Know About

Capital Funds Campaigns

Why You Would Be Enlisted

If the leadership of an organization's capital-funds campaign wants to enlist you as a volunteer solicitor, it is probably because you are active in the organization's affairs, are known to be effective in fund raising, and are deemed capable of asking for the substantial commitments a capital campaign requires.

Whether you agree to serve will depend upon whether you have sufficient interest in the organization, believe in the objectives of the campaign, and want to make the necessary effort to help achieve them.

A major organization is lucky if it has on its board even several individuals who are capable of asking for pledges of $100,000 or more. Not many organizations have more than a few board members equal to the task of soliciting commitments of from $25,000 to $50,000.

Therefore, if you do not flinch from an assignment to solicit pledges for substantial amounts, your services as a volunteer should be highly desirable to an organization, whether you are on its board or are otherwise associated with it.

What a Volunteer Solicitor Should Know About

Why Capital Funds Are Needed

The gift-supported organization you decide to serve is probably like many others: it needs capital funds periodically for construction, for endowment, or for construction and endowment. These two needs are usually coupled because a new building requires endowment for its maintenance.

Construction funds may be needed for a new building; or for an addition to, or renovation of, an existing structure. They are termed "expendable funds," since they are expected to be used up in meeting construction costs.

Funds for construction work that entails only modest expenditure—such as the repair of a roof or the remodeling of a room—can usually be included in annual maintenance costs and therefore provided by the annual giving campaign.

Only the income from the investment of endowment funds is available to an organization; the income can be used either as donors stipulate or, if they do not stipulate, at the discretion of an organization's board. A board can invade the principal of quasi-endowment, which includes gifts for which the donors specify such use and even gifts that were given to the organization for no specific purpose and which the board treats as endowment. The principal of quasi-endowment funds is most often invaded to wipe out annual deficits.

The great need of almost every privately supported organization is for funds with no restrictions on their use, so that they can be applied where they are most needed at any particular time. However, since gifts of such funds are not always attractive to donors, institutions seeking endowment often feel compelled to accept restrictions and even to encourage them by creating endowment gift opportunities that have appeal for contributors.

How Capital Funds Are Raised

If your organization is well managed, it anticipates its capital needs and makes plans to meet them when they will be required. It

CAPITAL FUNDS CAMPAIGNS

launches a capital-funds campaign after it has thoroughly studied and firmed up its needs; and has learned, through an objective feasibility study conducted by a fund-raising counseling firm, that the prospects for achieving its projected campaign goal are realistic.

Capital campaign objectives can include expendable funds for purposes other than construction. The campaign goal can also incorporate the total annual giving funds estimated to be needed during the duration of the capital campaign; this practice, however, has by no means achieved general acceptance.

The dollar goals of capital campaigns have ranged from less than a million dollars to several hundred million dollars. Ordinarily, to meet such goals, a minimum of two years is required to obtain the necessary pledges from donors; and to encourage them to make the substantial pledges a capital campaign needs, donors are permitted to spread the payment of their pledges over a three-year period.

The size, rather than the number, of pledges is important in a capital campaign, since a relatively small number of donors (sometimes only 10 percent) often provides the lion's share (sometimes as much as 90 percent) of the total goal. This factor influences all activity of the campaign and accounts for its relatively unhurried pace.

Thus, ample time is taken to enlist the strongest possible volunteer leadership for the campaign; to attract and orient capable volunteer solicitors to serve under the campaign leaders; to cultivate thoroughly the major prospects before they are solicited; and to encourage such prospects to give thoughtful consideration to ways by which they could make their finest commitments.

It is essential to avoid setting arbitrary deadlines and rigidly following a pre-determined timetable, and to permit the campaign to advance purposefully and at whatever pace is required for the effective solicitation of the necessary pledges in the order of their importance.

For this reason, major prospects are not solicited until advance gift prospects are accounted for; special gift prospects are approached only after major gift prospects have made their pledges; and general gift prospects are asked to pledge after those capable of larger commitments have been seen. Adhering to this sequence in the solicitation of prospects has proved to be sound campaign strategy.

In recent decades, capital campaigns have been undertaken by many gift-supported institutions (mainly colleges) on an average of every 10 years. More recently, some institutions have started new capital campaigns on the very heels of the previous ones. What began as a "once in a lifetime" capital campaign (as it was termed not too many years ago by some organizations) has evolved within the past two decades into a series of successive capital campaigns or virtually a continuing capital development program.

What Is Different About a Capital Campaign

You may best be able to understand the capital funds campaign when it is compared with the annual giving campaign (as defined in Chapter 1). The capital campaign differs in these respects:
1. It strives to achieve a much larger goal (a goal of $1 million could be large for an annual giving campaign but small for a capital campaign).
2. It requires more—and more complex—pre-campaign planning (an annual giving campaign's advance planning is usually focused on the single need to raise annual operating funds).
3. It seeks much larger commitments (a pledge could be 20 times larger than an annual giving campaign gift, and often is much larger than that).
4. It is more concerned with the size of pledges than with the number of donors participating (an annual giving campaign is usually interested in involving as many donors as possible at whatever levels of giving they can participate).
5. It seeks pledges payable over a number of years (annual giving campaigns need current contributions).
6. It solicits commitments at more giving levels: advance, major, special, and general (many annual giving campaigns seek only special and general gifts, and few of them also solicit advance gifts).

CAPITAL FUNDS CAMPAIGNS

7. It extends the campaign period over two or more years (an annual giving campaign is necessarily confined to the current year).
8. It places more emphasis on tax advantages because it needs the larger commitments which such advantages help make possible (most annual gifts have modest tax benefits).
9. It encourages donors to give in more different ways, even through planned gifts (an annual giving campaign needs gifts that are available in the current year).
10. It provides for far greater cultivation of prospects to help assure that when they are solicited they will be ready to pledge at their best (an annual giving campaign's cultivation efforts are usually limited and modest).
11. It is more strict in requiring in-person solicitation of prospects because it seeks the largest pledges possible from donors capable of substantial commitments (the average annual giving campaign is not organized for in-person solicitation of any sizable group of prospects).
12. It often requires a volunteer solicitor to make more than one call on major prospects—to make sure they are considering the proper level of pledge, to provide them with whatever information and guidance they may need, and to allow them time to confer with their families and tax advisers (few solicitors for an annual giving campaign make even one call on an important prospect).
13. It makes greater use of named gift opportunities and other forms of donor recognition (not all annual giving campaigns offer these types of recognition).
14. It encourages donors more to indicate the purposes for which they want their gifts to be used (annual giving campaigns usually ask donors to contribute to general operating support).
15. It adheres to a more rigid sequence of prospect solicitation, starting with those with the greatest giving capacity and obtaining their pledges before moving on to those with the next largest potential (an annual giving campaign often seeks gifts from all levels of donors simultaneously).

What a Volunteer Solicitor Should Know About

16. It usually requires a larger and more complex volunteer structure and a larger professional staff (an annual giving campaign's requirements are far more modest).
17. It more often determines its goal with the aid of a feasibility study (an annual giving campaign goal is usually set arbitrarily by its leadership).
18. It calls for more careful selection of volunteer solicitors and more in-depth orientation of them (soliciting for an annual giving campaign is a far simpler assignment).
19. It often needs less publicity because the solicitation of major prospects can sometimes be more effective when only they are privy to the undertaking (an annual giving campaign needs more publicity because it seeks more—and more modest—contributors).

Because of these differences, your role as a volunteer solicitor for a capital campaign should be more difficult, more important, and therefore more personally satisfying than the role of a volunteer solicitor for an annual giving campaign.

What a Feasibility Study Provides

Through a competent and objective feasibility study, your organization can learn what it needs to know before embarking upon a capital funds campaign. It can gain such essential information as the following:

—The extent of the funds it could raise (feasible goal)
—The period of time needed to raise the goal (timetable)
—The type of effort that would be required (campaign plan)
—The sources of support and what each source could give
—The strength of the case for support of the campaign
—The availability of leaders, workers, and prospective donors
—The conditions that could advance the campaign's success
—The requirement for a cultivation program for prospects
—The appropriate volunteer structure for the campaign

CAPITAL FUNDS CAMPAIGNS

—The extent of the need for professional staff and counsel
—The cost of conducting the campaign (campaign budget)

The study to obtain this information could best be conducted by an experienced fund-raising counseling firm, which ordinarily would hold in-person interviews with individuals whose advice, as well as understanding and support, could be important to the success of the proposed campaign.

The interviewees would include board members, volunteer members of important committees, professional staff members, major donors to previous capital and annual giving campaigns, corporate executives, foundation officers, government officials, and any others who could provide needed guidance or support.

The views, opinions, and intentions of these individuals are analyzed and evaluated in the study, and they form the basis for the counseling firm's recommendations to the organization. When the goal is feasible, the study recommends that the campaign be undertaken; when the goal is not realistic, the study may recommend that a smaller goal be adopted or that the campaign be postponed until the organization can strengthen its fund-raising position.

How a Capital Campaign Is Structured

Your board leadership usually enlists the campaign's general chairman, who in turn makes all of the other volunteer appointments. He presides over a campaign steering committee which would set campaign policies and oversee the efforts of the other campaign committees.

Several influential board members usually assist the general chairman in soliciting pledges from the other board members. Pledges from board members, who are expected to give first and set the example for all other prospective donors, usually provide most of the advance gifts to form a nucleus fund—a substantial portion of the goal to assure that the campaign is launched under favorable auspices.

Separate campaign committees are usually designated to solicit major gifts (the largest after the pace-setting advance gifts), special gifts (the next largest), and general gifts (the smallest). An evaluations committee could be appointed, though the function of rating the giving potential of prospects could best be assumed by the committees that would solicit the prospects.

How a Capital Campaign Is Staffed

If your organization is like most, it staffs its capital campaign in one of three ways. Its development department personnel provides professional campaign direction, with or without fund-raising counsel; a fund-raising counseling firm is engaged and its members furnish resident campaign direction; or a search is undertaken (often with the help of fund-raising counsel) to find an experienced campaign director to work directly for the organization and to recruit a campaign staff.

How the Campaign Goal Is Determined

While a feasibility study indicates the extent of the funds that your organization is likely to be able to raise, it can recommend a larger or "stretch" goal—one that would challenge prospective donors to contribute more than they might ordinarily give.

A "stretch" goal, however, should not strain the credibility of prospective donors in the goal's achievement. Understandably, donors like to believe—and often will not give if they do not believe—that a goal can be attained.

The board of your organization, of course, determines the campaign goal. In making its determination, the board can follow or disregard the feasibility study's recommendations.

The boards of some organizations often decide to try to achieve a goal even though it has been judged unfeasible; or to adopt a goal which is not feasible in the usual capital campaign period of from two to three years, and to attempt to attain it by extending the duration of the campaign for as long as the effort may require.

CAPITAL FUNDS CAMPAIGNS

How the Campaign Timetable Is Set

The timetable for a capital campaign ordinarily allows for a minimum of two years for the solicitation of pledges. It provides time periods for each of the usual campaign phases (advance, major, special, and general); and the length of each phase is determined by the organization's (or the feasibility study's) estimate of the time it could take to obtain the needed pledges.

Once the campaign is launched, however, the timetable should be made to conform to the realities of the situation. Thus, if more time is required for any particular phase, that phase should be extended and the timetable adjusted to accommodate the extension.

How Prospects Are Scheduled for Solicitation

The solicitation of prospects in a capital campaign starts with those who can make the largest pledges and ends with those who can give the least. The order of solicitation, then, is advance, major, special, and general prospects.

It is important in a capital campaign to complete the solicitation of one phase before beginning the next phase; in that way, some control can be exercised over the level of gifts it seeks. Otherwise, if it becomes known that smaller gifts are welcomed, some prospects who could pledge more could be tempted to give "early and less."

How Gift Levels Are Suggested to Donors

In a capital campaign, as in an annual giving campaign, there are two devices available to you as a solicitor to indicate to prospects the level of gift that is desired of them. They are recognition categories and gift opportunities.

Donor recognition categories are established for those who pledge at specified levels. These categories often include benefactor, patron, and sponsor; and the range of gifts they encompass in a multi-million dollar campaign could extend from $25,000 to $1,000,000 and more.

What a Volunteer Solicitor Should Know About

Named gift opportunities are also offered at various levels. Donors are given the opportunity to have their names, or the names of those they wish to honor or memorialize, associated with a wide range of physical facilities (which could include an entire building or the smallest room in it) or with a variety of programs that could be endowed.

If you cannot use either of these relatively painless ways of suggesting the level of commitment you seek from your prospects, there is little likelihood of giving them offense—and a distinct advantage in avoiding any misunderstanding—if you simply tell them what the organization hopes they would consider. They would probably like to know.

What Sources of Support To Solicit

A capital campaign solicits all appropriate sources of support, including individuals, foundations, corporations, and government. Each of these sources differ in their interests and in the extent of commitments they prefer to make.

Usually, individual prospects provide most of the campaign goal; corporations contribute relatively little and are not inclined to commit funds beyond the current year; foundations generally confine their support to programs (preferably new programs); and government is not inclined to give to construction or endowment.

How the Case for the Campaign Is Made

The case or rationale for a capital campaign, while usually less simple than that of an annual giving campaign, should not be complex; if it is to be understandable and convincing to prospects, it should be conceptually clear and uncomplicated.

With a capital campaign that seeks funds for construction and endowment, the projected construction should be shown as filling a need which cannot be met more effectively by other means, all of which were thoroughly studied. The need for endowment should also be convincingly demonstrated—whether it is for the mainte-

CAPITAL FUNDS CAMPAIGNS

nance of a new building, the support of a new program or service, or an increase in current operating costs.

As a volunteer solicitor, you will want to understand and be able to explain to your prospects the need for the campaign objectives. You will also want to be familiar with the campaign plan, so that you will know how your role fits into the overall campaign scheme.

What Guidance You Can Expect

Your guidance as a volunteer solicitor should include both briefings and written materials. Briefings could be provided by the chairman of the committee you are asked to join, or by the professional campaign director. The campaign materials could include:

—A case statement, prepared as a typwritten presentation or printed brochure, which can be given to a prospect
—A one-page outline of the case for your use in talking with a prospect
—A folder listing the various ways a prospect can give and their tax advantages
—A guide offering suggestions for soliciting prospects
—A question-and-answer sheet, addressing the questions prospects are most likely to ask, for your guidance
—A list of named gift opportunities from which you can select those of particular interest to your prospects
—An architectural rendering of a new building or addition to the organization's present facility (assuming new construction is a campaign objective)

How You Are Assigned Prospects

If you are asked to join a campaign soliciting committee (such as a special gifts committee), it would be because the campaign leadership believes that you are capable of soliciting pledges at the level that that committee is seeking.

After you have been appropriately briefed on the work of the

What a Volunteer Solicitor Should Know About

committee, you would be requested to review a list of prospective donors (which is usually prepared by the organization's development department), note the prospects you know, and provide any information on them which would be helpful in determining their philanthropic interests and giving patterns.

You would be urged to suggest any additions to the prospect list. And you would certainly be asked to indicate the prospects (among those you know) whom you would be willing to solicit.

What You Should Know About Your Prospects

You have, of course, a far better chance of succeeding with prospects whom you know than with strangers. For one thing, you have no problem in arranging to see them. For another, you know something about their philanthropic interests.

But you may not be aware of all of their charitable gifts—even of all their contributions to your organization. Its development department should possess this information.

You should receive from the department a profile of each of your prospects. It should include pertinent biographical data, a record of gifts to your organization, other services to your organization, important contributions to other causes, and special philanthropic interests.

This information should provide you with valuable guidance, for what prospects have given in the past furnishes some indication of the extent of their interest and ability to contribute in the future. And in the solicitation of prospects, it is important that they know you are informed of their previous gifts.

How Donors Can Pledge

When an organization undertakes a capital campaign for an ambitious goal, it may not be able to achieve its objective only with outright gifts of cash and securities. It therefore may have to accommodate to the financial situations of some donors, and accept other types of gift commitments.

CAPITAL FUNDS CAMPAIGNS

Such an organization may accept gifts of tangible personal property and real estate, and planned gifts. Planned gifts, including bequests and gifts of future interests (often incorrectly referred to as "deferred gifts"), may not be realized by the organization until some years after the conclusion of the campaign.

However, fund-raising experience has shown that even bequest programs start to pay off for an organization within five years; and some capital campaigns are now planned to run—or are extended to—five years, if not longer.

How the Tax Laws Benefit the Donor

Usually, prospective donors capable of making substantial capital commitments are kept informed by their tax advisers on the charitable deductions the tax laws permit. Occasionally, however, prospects have questions about the tax advantages of the various ways they can give to a campaign; and a solicitor could find it useful to be generally informed.

The income and estate tax laws that affect philanthropic giving are periodically changed. Therefore, the tax advantages shown here (as they existed in 1981) for the following types of gifts should be checked with your organization's tax expert:

Gifts of Money Donors take an income tax deduction for the amount of their gifts of up to 50% of their adjusted gross income, and carry over any excess to the next five years at the same percentage.

Appreciated Securities With long-term appreciated securities, the deduction is up to 30% of adjusted gross income, with a five-year carryover for any excess. Donors benefit from a deduction for the full market value and completely avoid any capital gains tax on appreciation. The deduction can be increased under certain conditions, which interested prospects may want to discuss with their tax advisers. With short-term appreciated securities, the deduction is limited to the securities' cost basis, and is up to 50 percent of adjusted gross income with a five-year carryover for any excess. There is no tax on the appreciation.

Tangible Personal Property and Real Estate A gift of tangible personal property is generally deductible to the extent of its fair market value, reduced by 40 percent of the long-term capital gain that would have resulted if it had been sold at its fair market value. Consult your tax advisor for variations to this rule. The deduction for real estate is the same as for appreciated securities.

Planned Gifts Among these gifts, which include gifts of future interests, are charitable income trusts, charitable remainder trusts, life insurance policies naming charitable organizations as ultimate beneficiaries, and bequests. The tax advantages of these gifts vary. A planned gift can provide donors with income for life. A gift of future interest of highly appreciated but low-yielding securities or real estate can be converted into higher-yielding investments to provide more spendable income for the donor, who avoids long-term capital gains and qualifies for a charitable tax deduction in the year the gift is made. The organization is served because it eventually receives the principal of such gifts.

Why In-Person Solicitation Is Essential

It has already been noted that in-person solicitation is the most effective way of seeking substantial gifts. And if that is true of the annual giving campaign, it is even more true of the capital campaign.

That is because in a capital campaign, prospects are solicited for far greater contributions; and because those who are considered prospects for such substantial commitments ordinarily have shown more than a casual interest in the organization.

A meeting with such prospects to ask them to give thoughtful consideration to a substantial pledge is therefore appropriate, as well as essential. Indeed, more than one meeting may be needed. This requirement has perhaps been best stated by the late Harold J. Seymour, a consultant who first articulated many of the concepts that inform present-day fund raising.

Seymour has said that if a solicitor asks major prospects for pledges and obtains them on the first visit, the solicitor has failed in not asking for enough. If the solicitor had asked for larger pledges (which the capital campaign needs and the prospects could make),

CAPITAL FUNDS CAMPAIGNS

the prospects would have needed more time to consider such pledges and to discuss them with their families and their tax advisers.

As a solicitor, you will probably have to meet more than once with major prospects to obtain their finest pledges. The result of any attempt to achieve your objective in one visit could undoubtedly be far less than what your prospects could potentially pledge.

When Donors Pledge at Their Best

Donors usually make the finest pledges of which they are capable when they fully understand and appreciate the importance of the campaign's objectives and the need for their realization. Other factors, however, are also influential.

Prospective donors should be helped to recognize that they are being asked for a pledge, not a gift. A gift usually implies the use of funds currently available, while a pledge is payable over three or more years. What a capital campaign needs of donors is the level of pledges they would require three or more years to pay.

Another factor that encourages prospects to pledge generously is to know that, in the event future developments prevent them from fulfulling their pledges, the organization would not press them legally for payment. Except for special cases of donors who are very elderly or who request certain recognition, it is usually advisable for an organization to avoid legally binding pledges. Prospects, however, should be made to understand that the organization expects them to make pledges with the conscientious intention of fulfilling them.

Named gift opportunities, which offer attractive recognition and match the donors' own interests, could be a strong factor in raising their giving sights. Another factor is the desire of donors to achieve recognition as benefactors, patrons, or sponsors, which an organization may offer. A further factor is the inclination of donors to want to match the gifts of their peers.

Prospective donors could pledge more liberally if they are shown

What a Volunteer Solicitor Should Know About

how their total resources can be used—often with tax advantages for them—to meet their pledges. With prospects who would like to pledge more than their currently available resources permit, you could suggest pledges that can be paid through a combination of up-front gifts of cash and securities and of planned gifts—provided, of course, it is campaign policy to accept planned gifts.

What Role You Take in Planned Giving

As a solicitor, you do not have to be an expert on planned gifts. Your role is only to suggest that prospects consider a planned gift (your organization's planned giving adviser can tell you what types of gifts to suggest) when such gifts would enable them to make larger commitments.

Here are two examples, however, which may be helpful to you in understanding planned giving:
1. If your prospects cannot contribute substantially from capital, they may be interested in contributing the income from capital for 10 or more years—and thereby gain an income tax charitable deduction—through a charitable income trust.
2. If your prospects need the income from their capital, they may be interested in contributing capital to your organization and receiving for life the income from its investment—and thereby gain an immediate income tax charitable deduction—through a charitable remainder trust.

In the first example, your organization would receive income from the outset; in the second example, it would benefit ultimately. In both examples, the donors would benefit from tax deductions and your organization would gain funds it would otherwise not receive.

If your prospects are interested in making planned gifts, you or the organization's planned giving expert should suggest that they consult their own attorneys or tax advisers, who should approve the appropriateness of the suggested planned gifts for the donors and should handle the technical aspects of making the gifts.

CAPITAL FUNDS CAMPAIGNS

What General Guidelines To Observe

There are probably no capital campaigns that realistically can identify more prospects for substantial pledges than they need to achieve their goals. Most campaigns do not have so many prospects at this level that they can afford to have even one of them solicited ineffectively.

Your basic approach as a solicitor, therefore, should be to take whatever time you may need, or feel is required, with prospects capable of substantial support—to encourage and assist them in making the finest pledges their means may permit.

Any departure from this approach can succeed only in rushing prospects into making commitments and in receiving only a token of what they are capable of giving. And the receipt of a token gift is not only a disappointment but also a loss of a potentially important contribution.

As a solicitor, you should seek from your prospects pledges which are generous and proportionate (in proportion to the amount of the campaign goal and the extent of their means). It is important to focus all prospects' giving sights at the highest levels their resources permit.

Capital campaign prospects are usually among those who contribute to an organization's annual giving campaign. If your organization accords number one priority to annual giving, you should ask your donors for capital commitments over and above what they contribute to annual giving.

What To Learn on Your First Visit

Assume that a prospect assigned to you is a man capable of making a substantial capital commitment if he is properly solicited. Your initial visit with your prospect should enable you to acquaint him with the objectives of the campaign and the need for substantial pledges to realize them, and to learn how he feels about your organization and how he reacts to the campaign objectives.

If you learn that the prospect is not sufficiently interested or cultivated to pledge at the desired level, you should not press him. Instead, you should arrange with your organization to involve him in those of its activities which may interest him, and to cultivate him in general until such time as he may be ready to pledge at his best.

If your prospect is ready, you should note whether any of the campaign objectives are of particular interest to him; if so, you may be able subsequently to match several named gift opportunities with his interests. You should also endeavor to learn specifically whether his financial situation could prevent him from making an adequate commitment of cash or securities over a three-year period.

Conclude the first meeting by indicating to the prospect the level of pledge you hope he would consider; and mention your own commitment, for that could be more persuasive than almost anything else you can tell him. Leave him with appropriate campaign material, and with the suggestion that he think about what he would like to pledge until you call on him again.

After the visit, you should consult with the chairman of your campaign committee if you need assistance with any problem you may have encountered. You may feel that you are not the right person to pursue the solicitation, or that another volunteer should accompany you on the next visit. You may need to suggest a combination of outright and planned gifts—if planned gifts are acceptable—that would meet the prospect's particular financial situation if he is to pledge generously.

You can expect help on all such problems from the chairman of your campaign committee, the campaign professional staff, and the organization's planned giving expert.

What To Achieve on Subsequent Visits

With the insights gained from your first visit with the prospect, you should be prepared to advance the solicitation purposefully on the second visit. Specifically, you should be armed with whatever information the prospect may need to decide on his commitment.

CAPITAL FUNDS CAMPAIGNS

If he has previously indicated any special interests, show him several gift opportunities matching his interests which are set at amounts to which he might aspire.

If his financial situation presents a problem, offer him the suggested combination of outright and planned gifts he could pledge which you devised with the help of your campaign advisers.

Your prospect may have other questions which occurred to him since your first meeting, or which came up during his discussions with his family or tax adviser. If you don't have the answers, promise to get them for him promptly.

These answers may be the main subject of a third visit, unless the prospect wants them as soon as possible by telephone. The important notion to convey to the prospect is that you want him to give thoughtful consideration to the level of pledge that the campaign needs and that he could take pride in.

How a Pledge Should Be Confirmed in Writing

As soon as your prospect informs you that he has decided on his pledge, ask him to confirm it in writing at once. You should have a simple pledge form with you, and suggest that he use it—or adapt it as he or his attorney may wish.

This form could simply state that the donor is writing to confirm his pledge of $_____ toward the achievement of the $__ million goal of the (organization), and that he expects to make payment (in types of gifts such as cash or securities) over a period of ____ years.

The form could also indicate the schedule of payments the donor expects to make (which is usually one payment for each of three years), and it could request that he be notified when payments are due. The average form concludes with the statement that the donor understands that his payments will be tax deductible to the full extent authorized by law.

A donor who is reluctant to sign a pledge can be asked to sign a statement of intent which need differ from the pledge form only in one respect: it would substitute "It is my intention to contribute $_____." for "I pledge $_____."

In asking the donor to confirm his pledge or intention in writing promptly, you can explain that by doing so he will enable the campaign to count his commitment toward the achievement of the goal, and to use it to show campaign progress and thus encourage others to make their commitments.

Even if pledges are not legally binding, they indicate to the executors of an estate that the donors did make the pledges and intended to honor them. More than a few organizations have lost millions of dollars because donors made oral pledges and did not live to confirm them in writing.

How To Acknowledge a Pledge

As the solicitor, you should be the first to know of your donor's pledge or should be told of it promptly; and you should be among the first to thank him. Even if you thank the donor in person or by telephone, you should also send him a thoughtful letter of appreciation.

While your organization must have established a procedure for responding to a donor's pledge, you should not hesitate to make sure that every pledge you account for is promptly and gratefully acknowledged. Letters of appreciation are usually sent by the campaign chairman and, when appropriate, by the organization's president or board chairman.

With payments on pledges (which are tax deductible), the treasurer should send the donor an official receipt form for use with his federal tax return. It is advisable that a letter of appreciation from an appropriate officer precede the printed receipt form, which in itself is not an adequate initial response to the donor.

You should also make certain that any of your prospects who contribute to the campaign are accorded every recognition to which their gifts entitle them. That recognition could be a donor designation (such as benefactor, patron or sponsor); or the association of the donor's name with a gift opportunity.

CAPITAL FUNDS CAMPAIGNS

How Pledges Can Be Increased

No matter how effectively you solicit your prospects, some of them will pledge less than their means permit. Your response, of course, should be to thank them sincerely for whatever they have pledged; they will know, from the giving level you suggested to them previously, that they pledged less than what the organization hoped they would give.

It could be valuable to maintain contact with donors whose pledges disappoint you, as well as with donors whose pledges meet your expectations. You could do this by keeping them posted on the progress of the campaign, and on the use that is being made of contributions like theirs.

Through such continuing communication, these donors could develop a deeper interest in the campaign and could increase their pledges. It is a sound fund-raising adage that the best prospects for gifts are those who have already given. If kept interested, these donors often give more.

When You Don't Know the Answer

The possibility of a solicitor not knowing the answer to a question a prospect may ask is certainly more likely in a capital campaign than in an annual giving campaign, because a capital campaign usually is far more complex and often involves more technical information (such as on planned gifts and on their tax advantages).

There is certainly no reason for a solicitor to be other than honest in admitting he does not know the answer to a difficult question; he has only to promise to get the information for the prospect. In cases where the subject is complicated, it could be advisable to bring the prospect together with a representative of your organization who can speak authoritatively on the matter.

What Role Publicity Can Play

Publicity in a capital campaign can be effective only when an organization knows when to use it, when not to use it, and how to use it.

In the early stages of a campaign, publicity is usually inadvisable because prospects for the advance or major gifts are often more effectively solicited before the campaign has "gone public" and when they feel that they are among the very few who are privy to it.

In the latter stages when larger numbers of prospects are solicited for smaller pledges, favorable publicity about the campaign (such as its progress in advancing toward its goal) can lend support to the solicitation effort and help maintain the momentum of a campaign.

In a capital campaign, since most of the pledges usually come from members of an organization's constituency, well-planned publicity in the mass media can serve to encourage and enthuse the donors and workers by making them realize that the case for the campaign is bigger than the organization and that its importance extends beyond its constituency.

Publicity can also provide public acknowledgement of donors' substantial commitments and, in the process, encourage them to increase their pledges. It can also accord public recognition to volunteer leaders and outstanding workers for their efforts in behalf of the campaign.

Campaign publicity should include internal and external publicity. Internal publicity is intended to keep the leaders and workers informed on campaign progress and developments, and to provide them with new information; such information can be conveyed by a periodically published campaign bulletin. When the whole constituency is to be solicited, a campaign newsletter can be issued to keep all members of the constituency informed and interested, and to lay the groundwork for their solicitation.

External publicity is aimed at the general public through the mass media, including newspapers, magazines, and television and radio. It is also aimed at the specific publics which could be important to an organization, which could include members of other organizations which have similar interests.

CAPITAL FUNDS CAMPAIGNS

Why Fund-Raising Costs Should Not Be a Problem

The fund-raising costs of organizations' annual giving campaigns can approach 30 percent and still be "reasonable," in the view of the National Information Bureau, as stated in Chapter 1. The costs of capital fund campaigns, however, are usually far below such a percentage; they could average about 5 percent, assuming that the institutions have a supportive constituency and do not need to create one.

For this reason, the average capital campaign should not experience any special problems with the acceptance of its fund-raising costs. While these costs will be higher in amount than the average annual giving campaign's and will extend over more than one year, they will be proportionately lower when compared to the total funds raised.

3

What a Volunteer Leader Should Know About

Fund Raising in General

How a Volunteer Leader Is Defined

Many a gift-supported organization labors under the misconception that fund raising is a completely separate activity and that it can succeed without reference to other organizational functions.

The success of an organization's fund-raising efforts usually reflects its success in advancing its program, serving its constituency, managing its financial resources, and keeping the community informed on its activities and stewardship.

There is a simple reason for this relatedness: to raise funds effectively and continually, an organization must be able to show that it merits support. Donors may often give emotionally and certainly in response to those who solicit them; ultimately, however, donors give substantially and consistently to organizations whose programs are effectively and efficiently administered.

For fund-raising purposes, therefore, a volunteer leader is defined in this book as anyone who assumes a volunteer position of responsibility, in an annual giving or capital-funds campaign, which is at a level above that of a solicitor (recognizing, of course, that campaign leaders also take solicitation assignments).

What a Volunteer Leader Should Know About

A volunteer leader is also anyone whose role with an organization can affect its fund raising. Such a leader could therefore be the chairman, or a member, of any of these groups:
—A board (of trustees or directors), because it is central to the success of any fund-raising effort the organization undertakes;
—A nominating committee, because it can strengthen a board by identifying and proposing for membership individuals who can add to a board's fund-raising capability;
—A finance or budget committee, because it can help an organization make maximum use of its gift income, which can be a persuasive reason for donors' continuing support; and
—An investment committee, because it can enable an organization to point with pride to the return from the investment of its present endowment funds, which can attract more endowment.

While these committees are significantly related to an organization's fund-raising capability, the board's relationship is the most vitally important. It is therefore relevant to note why many boards are not strengthened and to indicate how they could be strengthened.

Why Boards Are Not Strengthened

The boards of many gift-supported organizations are not strengthened for at least 10 reasons that come to mind.

1. The chairman of a board consciously or unconsciously does not want it strengthened, for that would threaten his position. This is particularly true of boards which have had essentially the same members, and the same chairmen, for many years. There might be some value in this policy if such boards were strong and effective, but this is ordinarily not the case.

2. A board fails to establish—or observe—a term of office for its members or a limit on the number of times its members can be reelected. This failure serves to perpetuate the same board membership. Such a board does not recognize—or is not concerned—that its members become tired sooner or later (which is why all boards need the renewal and revitalization that come from a periodic infusion of new members).

3. A board believes that the number of its members is firmly set for

FUND RAISING IN GENERAL

all time in its by-laws and incorporation papers. It fails to appreciate that there is nothing magical about this number or difficult about enlarging it.

4. A board wants to remain small so that it can be a working board. It certainly should know that committees do the work of an organization, and that a board has time only to act on the recommendations of committees—to approve of the recommendations, to disapprove of them, to amend them, or to send them back to the committees for more work.

5. A board does not understand how a nominating committee should function. It thinks the committee should nominate a candidate for the board only when there is a vacancy. It does not see the committee's mission as a continuing search for individuals who could be valuable nominees.

6. A board is not clear or equally concerned about all of its primary purposes. These purposes are to set basic policy, discharge its fiscal responsibilities, provide for the organization's financial support, and hire and fire the professional director. Least attention seems to be accorded financial support.

7. A board is timid about raising the level of its membership by seeking to enlist individuals of higher economic or social status, or is limited in its capacity to enlist such individuals and cannot devise a mechanism for reaching above its level.

8. A board does not recognize that it is central to the success of all fund raising that is undertaken, and that its strength determines the organizations' fund-raising effectiveness.

9. Many board members do not like to raise funds, do not really approve of fund raising, and view with some misgiving the addition of new board members who are capable of raising funds.

10. A board does not know how to enlist individuals of importance and means even when opportunities occur. Its leaders cannot make an effective case for board membership, and they often lack the courage to spell out the board's financial responsibilities.

How To Strengthen a Board

For its guidance, an organization should establish criteria for board membership. The traditional criteria of "wealth, wisdom, and work" still have merit. Every board member should not have to meet all three criteria, but each member should be able to meet at least one, and preferably two, of them.

As long as organizations continue to have to meet increasingly larger annual budgets (as well as periodic capital needs), they should enlist adequate numbers of board members with sufficient "wealth" to contribute substantially themselves and to be able to solicit effectively other prospects for sizable gifts. Not every member who can give can get support. But the capacity to give often includes the ability to get.

In planning to strengthen its board for fund raising, an organization should understand that its board should be representative of all of the sources to which it wishes to apply for financial support. For example, if an organization wants support from labor unions, its board should include an influential labor leader.

An organization that wants its board to achieve a higher level of effectiveness should try to enlist those who could best enable it to meet its responsibilities. Too often, organizations focus on those whom its members know and think they can enlist without difficulty.

Once desirable nominees for the board are identified, they should be told not only the perquisites of board members but also the financial and fiscal responsibilities. Intelligent nominees want to know what they are letting themselves in for, and respect organizations which make this clear at the outset. Indeed, any attempt to underestimate or disguise the financial obligation of board membership does the nominee and the organization a serious disservice.

An organization should establish sufficient committees not only to do its work but also to serve as training grounds for volunteer leaders and feeders for the board. Committees will benefit, of course, by the inclusion of individuals with board potential.

Organizations should observe a rotation policy by which they "rotate off" the board those members who possess no further usefulness. Too often, leadership is afraid of hurting the feelings of a board member; and as a result, a position on the board is wasted for an additional term—a position which otherwise could have been filled by one who could serve usefully.

FUND RAISING IN GENERAL

An organization should insist that the whole board periodically participate in the identification and enlistment of desirable nominees. This effort is usually limited to the few members of a nominating committee. Advantage should be taken of the suggestions and the contacts of all board members.

A nominating committee should make certain in advance that all of the nominees would consider the organization at least among their top philanthropic priorities, and that they had served usefully and conscientiously in other organizations or community endeavors.

An organization should not hesitate to enlarge its board. A large board has an advantage over a small board; and with care, the quality of such a board can be retained. The Children's Hospital Medical Center in Boston used to have a Board of Trustees and a Board of Incorporators, with 125 members each; but even its recently combined Board of Trustees enables over 200 volunteer leaders to enjoy a top-level relationship with the Center and to feel a special call on their advocacy and support.

Once a board is strengthened, its chairman should make sure that it retains the interest (and thereby the support) of its new members. Interest at board meetings can be assured if they are planned as if the members were major gift prospects (as, in effect, some of the members are).

How Much Volunteer Leaders Should Know

Obviously, volunteer leaders should know more about annual giving and capital-funds campaigns than volunteer solicitors need to know. The contents of Chapters 1 and 2, as well as this one, have been determined accordingly.

However, more information than volunteer solicitors usually have to know about annual giving and capital funds campaigns has been included in the first two chapters. This was done intentionally, on the assumption that the more volunteer solicitors know about a campaign, the more effectively they can serve.

Therefore, there is much material in these two chapters that volunteer leaders should read to augment the information in this chapter, which is more closely related to the special problems and concerns that ordinarily confront volunteer leadership.

How Annual Giving Can Be Improved

While an annual giving campaign committee should plan and conduct the year's fund-raising effort, the board leadership can play an important role in helping to increase the campaign's effectiveness. Specifically, it can
—Enlist a strong campaign chairman;
—Assist the campaign chairman in forming a strong committee;
—Urge the campaign committee to undertake an ambitious goal;
—Press the committee to make in-person solicitation calls on donors capable of substantial gifts;
—Establish the policy that, whatever fund-raising efforts may be simultaneously pursued, prospective donors should be asked to make annual giving their number one priority;
—Pledge all board members (not just those on the campaign committee) to participate in the campaign by contributing generously and taking solicitation assignments; and
—Insist that the quality and effectiveness of mail appeals be periodically critiqued and improved.

Volunteer solicitors are only human, and many (if not most) of them will succumb to the temptation to write prospects rather than see them in person—for the simple reason that it is easier to send a letter than to make a visit. Accordingly, such volunteers will want—or appreciate—sample letters they can use or adapt.

The preparation of appeal letters is the responsibility of an organization's development department. "Guidelines for Mail Appeal" (Appendix B) can be used as a checklist by professionals in planning a mail-appeal effort and drafting suggested appeal letters.

This guide is appended because it can also serve the volunteer leaders who are called upon to approve mail appeal efforts and to sign appeal letters to past and prospective donors who are not solicited in person. It can provide them with a basis for judging the soundness of

FUND RAISING IN GENERAL

proposed mail-appeal efforts and the likely effectiveness of the appeal letters they are asked to sign.

Volunteer leaders are also called upon to approve and sign proposals requesting grants from foundations. The "Procedure for Making a Foundation Request" (Appendix C) is a checklist for preparing a foundation proposal. It can be used by professionals in drafting a proposal, and by volunteer leaders who sign proposals in evaluating their likely effectiveness.

When an organization's annual giving results remain the same for a number of years, the Board should consider engaging fund-raising counsel to learn through a study why the campaign returns have not increased and how they could be improved. Such a study could indicate how donors could be upgraded, and how additional donors could be attracted.

An established organization, particularly if its program has remained unchanged over a long period of time, could find it useful and probably beneficial to undertake a professionally guided self-study to determine whether its original objectives are still relevant; and, if they are, whether they are being effectively advanced.

A privately supported social agency in an urban area could find that it has not sufficiently related its services to the problems of the inner city. How an agency in the private sector can focus more funds and leadership on these problems is developed in Appendix D.

How a Telethon Should Be Considered

Some charitable organizations raise annual funds by sponsoring a telethon. Volunteer leaders should recognize that a telethon is not appropriate for every organization, and it is certainly not a substitute for the hard work that fund raising entails.

Before your organization decides to sponsor a telethon, it should be able to answer satisfactorily these seven questions, which illuminate the scope of the project and the organization's readiness for such an undertaking:
  1. Is the public exposure of a telethon in keeping with your organization's cause and character?

2. Does your organization's cause lend itself to visual presentation that would be dramatically effective?
3. Does your organization's cause concern a significant percentage of the locality, and is its leadership representative of the levels of the community that are important to the organization?
4. Does your organization have the large body of committed volunteers that a telethon would require, and have—or have access to—professional experts with telethon experience?
5. Will a television station in your locality make available from 15 to 20 hours of broadcasting time (usually from Saturday night through all day Sunday)?
6. Can your organization enlist the services of a well-known personality to act as master of ceremonies for a telethon?
7. Will your organization recognize that the project requires a complete fund-raising campaign within the telethon format, and will it assume the responsibility for such a campaign?

While the costs of producing a telethon will vary with the particular locality, the expenditures involved will be an important consideration. The soundest policy—and certainly the safest—is for an organization to raise in advance gifts the total costs of the telethon.

That advice is given to organizations considering a telethon by Norman H. Kimball, Director of Public Relations and Fund Raising for United Cerebral Palsy of New York, who has planned and conducted many telethons for his own organization and a number of others.

Kimball estimates that costs can run from 35 to 40 percent in the first few years. For his own organization's most recent telethon, which raised $1,600,000, the costs totaled $350,000.

In addition to the solicitation of advance gifts to cover the telethon's costs, Kimball also urges the use of pre-telethon mass mailings to donors, including "lapsed" donors, and to prospective donors; he considers such mailings not so much a solicitation as an alert that calls attention to the upcoming telethon. Advance gifts, as well as those phoned in during the event, are announced during the telethon.

Radiothons should be weighed with basically the same considerations in mind. The main difference is whether your organization's cause lends itself to effective auditory presentation.

FUND RAISING IN GENERAL

How Memberships Affect Fund Raising

Many nonprofit organizations have members whose annual dues help support annual operations. They may be organizations whose activities are limited to their members, such as the Council on Foreign Relations, or institutions that offer their members special privileges but whose activities are open to the general public, such as The Museum of Modern Art.

Organizations created memberships to attract both kindred spirits and financial support. But today, membership dues, like other sources of income, generally do not provide sufficient funds to meet the annual budget. Many an organization must now appeal to its members for annual contributions, in addition to their annual dues, to avert deficits.

Such an organization has no choice but to turn to its members for this additional support, for they are the most interested and devoted supporters it has and therefore the most promising prospects for annual gifts (although it must also appeal to all other potential prospects).

But it is often difficult to make a strong case for an annual contribution to members whose annual dues may be several hundred or even several thousand dollars. It is necessary to indicate to these members that, while the highest level of dues is very supportive indeed, the total income from all levels of dues provides only a portion (sometimes a small portion) of the total budget.

Such members should also be reminded that most of the members pay much more modest dues; and that the perquisites of membership represent a cost to the organization, so that the full dues are not available for the organization's annual upkeep. A museum, for example, has determined that the first $50 of a member's dues must be considered as quid pro quo—for the services a member is provided—and that only what he pays above that amount can be considered a contribution.

These explanations should help with the problem, but they have not yet solved it because many members apparently feel that their dues are—or should be—the extent of their annual support.

When an organization embarks on a capital-funds campaign, it has

71

the further problem of persuading its members of the need to make capital commitments over and above what they contribute through their dues and their annual gifts.

What Precedes a Capital Campaign

A board should undertake a capital-funds campaign only when the organization is functioning effectively and efficiently. (If this is not the case, the campaign should be put off until the organization is in a strong position.)

There are, in addition, two special requirements that a board should meet in advance of launching a capital campaign. One is to identify and firm up its capital needs; the other is to engage an outside fund-raising counseling firm to conduct a feasibility study.

In undertaking a capital campaign, an organization has to be in a position to be able to assure its potential donors that it has thoroughly studied the capital needs it seeks, that they are important and urgently required, and that they cannot be met more effectively in any other way.

The board of an organization, which usually authorizes a capital campaign, has the obligation of assuring itself that the projected goal is feasible within the time period the organization wants to devote to fund raising. This assurance can best be obtained by a professional fund-raising firm that has the capability and experience to conduct an objective feasibility study to determine the organization's fund-raising potential.

How a Fund-Raising Counseling Firm Should Be Selected

The appropriate organizational official (the board chairman, the development committee chairman, or the designated campaign chairman) should select at least three firms to interview. These firms can be members of the American Association of Fund-Raising Counsel (which includes about 30 member firms) or any other firms on which the organization has had favorable reports; but all of them

FUND RAISING IN GENERAL

should subscribe (as member firms must) to the Association's Fair Practice Code (Appendix E).

Each firm chosen should be asked whether it would undertake a feasibility study as a separate assignment, with no obligation on the part of the organization to retain its services if a campaign should be indicated.

Each firm should then be asked how it would plan the study, what the study would include, how many interviewees would be seen in person, what kind of a questionnaire would be used, what the written report would contain, when it would be completed, who would conduct the interviews and write the report, whether the firm would provide resident campaign direction or counseling if a campaign would be held, and what the cost of the study would be in terms of professional fees and out-of-pocket expenses.

In addition, each firm should be requested to provide as references the names of appropriate officials of somewhat similar organizations for which it also conducted feasibility studies and provided campaign counseling or resident direction. These references should be asked whether the firm provided a reasonable estimate of the fund-raising costs, how they would evaluate the firm's services, and whether they would engage the firm again for a similar feasibility study and campaign.

It is important to learn the extent of the experience of a firm's executives in campaign management, and to see the executive who would be in charge of planning and conducting the study and any of the firm's other professional personnel who would assist him.

After a firm is engaged, the organization has the right to read and approve of the study questionnaire the firm prepares for its use with interviewees; and to determine, with the firm's assistance, the individuals to be interviewed.

It is usually best to use the same firm for professional assistance with any campaign that may be subsequently undertaken, for it possesses the information and insights the study experience provided. It is therefore advisable to know in advance what type of campaign services the firm can provide and what it would be likely to cost.

One firm may offer resident campaign management: it makes available to the organization one or more of its members to provide day-to-day direction of the campaign on the organization's premises or at any other location the organization designates. Its senior firm members also furnish general advice and counsel as indicated.

Another firm may offer only campaign counseling: it advises and guides the campaign's volunteer leadership, as well as its fund-raising staff that mans the campaign office on a day-to-day basis. Such counseling is usually provided by a senior firm member.

Resident campaign management entails a higher fee but provides more personnel and assumes day-to-day responsibility; in addition, it relieves an organization of the need and the cost of enlarging its permanent staff.

Campaign counseling is economically advantageous for an organization which possesses a staff that can perform the routine campaign functions under a firm's oversight, and wants its staff to gain capital fund-raising capability through the campaign experience.

Why a Feasibility Study Is Essential

What a feasibility study provides (as outlined in Chapter 2) comprises the information that is vital for an organization to know in advance of undertaking a capital campaign. It indicates whether a campaign for the projected goal is feasible within a specified fund-raising period; and, if a campaign can be undertaken, how it can best be planned for maximum results.

The feasibility of a goal is usually determined by evaluating the strengths of these fund-raising factors: the case, leadership, workers, and prospects. While not all of these factors have to be equally strong, the overall evaluation should be one of sufficient strength for the requirements of the proposed campaign.

A related purpose of the study is to identify potential campaign leaders, workers, and prospects—particularly those who could assume the top campaign positions and those who could make the largest pledges. This information is essential in structuring and planning a campaign.

Another purpose of the study is to involve those who could be important to the success of a campaign in what could be considered an

FUND RAISING IN GENERAL

essential phase of the planning process. Their views are reflected in the study's recommendations, and this involvement provides some assurance of their subsequent support.

A further purpose of the study is to identify and evaluate any problems that could affect the course and outcome of a campaign, such as a serious public misconception of an organization's policy or the expectation that other organizations' campaigns could compete for the support of some of the same prospects. Knowing of such problems, as well as what to do about them, is important information for an organization to have before it makes a decision to launch a capital campaign.

Without the benefit of a feasibility study, a board could commit an organization to a capital campaign that could not succeed because its goal was unfeasible or because it was not planned effectively to overcome unforeseen obstacles. Such a campaign could prove expensive to an organization not only in terms of the funds and efforts it wastes but also in the discouragement and alienation of its supporters.

An example of the importance of investing in a feasibility study is the experience of a preparatory school that some years ago decided to economize by foregoing a study for a campaign to raise $400,000. After a year, the major prospects were solicited and their pledges totaled only $40,000. Fund-raising counsel was then consulted and it was learned that the prospects who pledged $40,000 were the only ones with the potential to give $350,000, and that the remaining prospects could provide at best only $50,000. The result was that the campaign was killed and the experience was damaging to the school.

How a Board Should Act on a Study Report

The written report of the study should contain at least these elements: a statement of the purpose of the study; the study findings (the views expressed by the interviewees); an analysis of the findings (the fund-raising counseling firm's evaluation of the participants' views); the firm's recommendations; and (if a campaign is feasible) a recommended campaign plan, timetable, and budget.

Usually, the first copies of the study report are submitted to an organization's volunteer and professional leaders, and the board chairman or the president indicates what other distribution should be made of the report. It is advisable to provide copies for at least all members of the board; and, in appropriate situations, to others who also participated as interviewees.

Interviewees have a right to know the results of a study to which they contributed their thinking. And the organization ordinarily has no reason to be concerned about any unfavorable findings, and every reason to be responsive to the participants' justifiable interest in the results. Indeed, this sharing of problems usually serves to strengthen a board.

Preferably, copies of the study report should be sent to board members sufficiently in advance of a board meeting to permit them to study the report carefully and be able to act upon it at the meeting. The board should be given ample opportunity at the meeting to discuss the report and ask questions about its contents before being requested to vote on its recommendations. The vote on a recommended capital campaign should be the instrument for the expression of the board's enthusiastic approval and support.

How a Campaign Goal Can Be Set

A feasibility study usually recommends a feasible or "stretch" goal. However, if the funds needed are far beyond what could be raised in the traditional campaign period of from two to three years, it could rcommend a capital development program that could extend as long as a decade.

An organization can undertake such a program to raise in three phases the total funds it will need over a 10-year period: the first phase for the most urgent needs could achieve the feasible goal; the second phase could seek the funds required for the next most urgent needs; and the third phase could meet the least urgent needs.

In determining a campaign goal, as was previously noted, the board of an organization can follow or disregard a feasibility study's recommendations. It should, however, seriously consider the recommendations since they reflect the giving intentions of its prospects for many of the larger pledges.

FUND RAISING IN GENERAL

But feasibility studies are not—and probably cannot be—exercises in scientific precision; and prospective donors' initial giving intentions can change, particularly in response to inspiring leadership. Consequently, some organizations have adopted campaign goals in excess of what studies found to be feasible—and they have succeeded in achieving them.

The problem with setting objectives that are recognizably unrealistic is that prospective donors prefer to contribute toward attainable goals.

Sometimes such "unfeasible" goals have been attained in the traditional campaign period, and other times they have required up to five years. The danger with longer campaign periods is the likelihood that leadership will tire and need to be replaced; interest and enthusiasm of solicitors will wane and require rekindling; and campaign momentum will sputter and have to be recharged.

When a board wants to try for a goal in excess of what a study indicates is feasible, it can take the total of its capital needs as a "working" goal and ask its advance gift prospects to contribute toward it. These lead commitments can usually indicate whether such a goal is realistic or whether the feasible goal should be subsequently adopted.

What Campaign Policies To Establish

If you are a member of a capital campaign's steering committee, you should be called upon at the outset to help set certain policies that will provide guidance for all volunteers and professionals involved in the conduct of the campaign.

One policy question—which concerns the size of the campaign goal—has been discussed previously because it usually is made by the board, acting on the feasibility study recommendation, rather than by the campaign steering committee which is subsequently appointed.

Another policy question—should pledges to the campaign be legally binding?—has been mentioned in Chapter 2 because of the effect it can have on prospects who are considering their commitments.

Since legally binding pledges can discourage prospective donors from making the generous commitments stretching into the future that a capital campaign needs to achieve its goal, pledges should not be legally binding except for special cases when important gift opportunities would be named and/or when the donor's age would indicate the advisability of having a claim on his estate.

Such a policy should make it clear that the organization assumes that the donor is making his pledge with the conscientious intention of fulfilling it, and that it would not press him for any remaining payments on a pledge that circumstances might prevent him from making.

A somewhat related question is: How many years should a donor be given to pay his pledge? When they are offered five years to pay, donors often pledge no more than they would if they were given only three years in which to make payments.

Donors should therefore be asked to make the most generous pledges they can pay over a three-year period. Then, should a donor's pledge fall short of expectations, he can be asked if he would increase his pledge proportionately by taking five years to pay.

The policy question—should named gift opportunities be offered to prospective donors?—ordinarily should be answered in the affirmative because of the value such opportunities have in indicating desired giving levels to prospects and in attracting major gifts.

Some institutions, however, may have standing policies that could preclude the offering of gift opportunities. Other institutions may be concerned about the appropriateness of named gift opportunities that might be developed for a campaign; if so, the campaign steering committee could reserve the right to approve gift opportunities before they are offered to prospects.

A closely related policy question—should recognition categories be established?—should also be answered affirmatively because these categories attract donors and help raise their giving sights, and enable an institution to give public recognition to donors of substantial gifts.

Customary recognition categories include benefactor, patron, sponsor, and donor (why they are most often used is explained in Appendix F). For campaign goals of about $2 million and $20 million, a campaign steering committee could consider these giving levels for such categories:

FUND RAISING IN GENERAL

	$2 Million Goal	**$20 Million Goal**
Benefactor	$100,000 and more	$500,000 and more
Patron	50,000 and more	100,000 and more
Sponsor	25,000 and more	50,000 and more
Donor	10,000 and more	25,000 and more

These giving levels are generally appropriate. In each campaign, however, the levels selected should have particular relevance to the individual institution, for there is no point in establishing giving levels to which prospects cannot aspire even if they extend themselves.

An important policy question is: what kinds of gifts should be accepted in the campaign? Gifts of cash and securities, of course, are always acceptable. Gifts of tangible personal property and real estate can have complications which an organization may not want—or be set up—to handle.

Planned gifts, including bequests and gifts of future interests, also represent a problem because campaigns usually prefer gifts that can be received in three years. Your campaign steering committee, however, may feel that the achievement of the campaign goal makes it advisable to accept planned gifts (such as a charitable remainder trust, a life insurance policy naming the institution as the ultimate beneficiary, and a bequest)—particularly if they are combined with whatever the donors could give outright in cash and securities.

Planned gifts may not be available by the date an institution wants to attain its campaign goal, but they may have other advantages. They could often represent gifts which would not otherwise have been made. And they would certainly be needed by an institution whenever they become available, since no capital campaign yet has provided a permanent solution to an institution's need for capital funds. A fuller examination of the advantages and possible dangers of accepting planned gifts in a capital campaign is provided in Appendix G.

When a Sponsoring Committee Should Be Considered

An organization that is going to launch a capital campaign often believes that it should organize a sponsoring committee comprised of individuals who, even though they may not be associated with the organization, would lend the campaign their endorsement.

If such an organization is local in scope, it enlists individuals in its locality who, by their endorsement, would show that the organization's campaign has community-wide support. If the organization has a national outreach, it asks prominent individuals throughout the country to indicate by their membership on a sponsoring committee that the organization is serving a national cause and that the campaign merits nation-wide support.

When they are enlisted, members of a sponsoring committee are usually asked only to endorse the campaign, with the understanding that whatever else they may want to do to further the campaign (such as making a contribution) would be optional on their parts. The names of members are listed on campaign stationery and literature, and are used in other appropriate ways.

The use of a sponsoring committee could be of particular value to an organization which feels that its own leadership is not sufficiently impressive or that it needs the benefit of community-wide or nation-wide endorsement.

How a Campaign Timetable Should Be Viewed

A campaign timetable is usually included in a feasibility study report when a campaign is recommended. Because of factors that cannot always be assessed precisely during the study, a timetable often proves to be overly optimistic, and a campaign runs longer than anticipated.

One reason is that the timetable is prepared in advance of the launching of a campaign, which can be delayed while the board comes to a decision on the recommended campaign or on the date to initiate it.

Another reason is the difficulty an organization can experience in enlisting campaign leadership. A further reason is the time required for advance gift prospects to be ready to pledge at their best.

This last reason has led to the recognition by professional fund raisers that contributors have their own timetables.

FUND RAISING IN GENERAL

Because of these and similar reasons, a timetable should be viewed as only an aid for campaign planning purposes, and should be revised as frequently as campaign conditions require. It must always allow sufficient time for the effective solicitation of prospects; otherwise, the campaign goal will not be achieved.

A timetable, which was prepared for a capital campaign projected over a 33-month period, is included for purposes of illustration as Appendix H.

Why Campaign Leadership Is Crucially Important

In structuring a capital campaign (as outlined in Chapter 2), the main concern should focus on leadership. A strong leader can make a weak structure productive; a weak leader can make a strong structure totter.

It has long been the view of many professional fund raisers that an aggressive businessman tends to make the most effective campaign chairman, because he can often do what does not seem possible. Thus, a lawyer (cited by contrast) tends to know all the reasons why something cannot be done; but a businessman does not know it cannot be done—so he does it. Actually, businessmen have made strong campaign chairmen, and so have lawyers.

There has also been the view in the past that women volunteers would not make effective campaign chairmen. This view has been exploded in recent years. Witness, for example, the successful capital campaigns for ambitious goals by such institutions as Smith College, The Museum of Modern Art, and the Los Angeles Music Center, which were led by women.

A strong campaign chairman is one who is respected and influential with the constituency; gives adequate time and first-class attention to the campaign's direction; makes a substantial gift and solicits other lead gifts; enlists capable volunteers for the other campaign positions; and sustains the spirit of the campaign organization when progress is slow or discouraging.

It is the campaign chairman who keeps the faith. And faith that success will ultimately be achieved is not easy to maintain throughout a long campaign that can be marked by arid spells, dashed expectations, and unforeseen disappointments. Yet faith can be essential to success, for what is believed can become a self-fulfilling prophesy.

The feasibility study report should provide the names of volunteers who, in the opinion of the interviewees who know them, could qualify best as campaign leaders.

How the Best Solicitors Should Be Used

If your organization is at all typical, it probably has too few volunteers who have the fund-raising ability to solicit pledges of $100,000 or more. Such volunteers should, of course, be enlisted to seek the larger advance gifts (as members of a campaign steering committee) and the major gifts (as members of a major gifts committee).

When the work of the latter committee is completed, these same solicitors will be needed to help solicit the largest special gifts, the next highest gift level. If they are not exhausted beyond resuscitation, they should be prevailed upon to lend this further assistance (as members of a special gifts committee).

To arrange for the maximum use of solicitors with the greatest fund-raising ability is the single most important step to be taken in structuring a campaign organization, for there are no others who can adequately substitute for them in soliciting prospects capable of substantial gifts.

Why Major Donors Should Be Made Solicitors

Donors who have made substantial pledges could be effective in asking others to contribute, and those donors who are willing to serve should be enlisted as solicitors. The interest of donors increases when they become involved in the campaign; and in persuading prospects to contribute, they often gain a greater awareness of the importance of the campaign and the feeling that they want to increase their own commitments.

FUND RAISING IN GENERAL

Donors who subsequently serve as solicitors sometimes find that they can pledge far more than they thought they could originally. Two instances come to mind. A woman who pledged $100,000 doubled her commitment, and then increased it by another $100,000, as a result of attending campaign committee meetings and being continually exposed to the need for more funds. And a man who pledged $10,000 first raised it to $50,000 (to be a patron) and finally increased it to $100,000 (to be a benefactor), mainly as a result of his efforts to persuade other donors to increase their pledges and qualify for higher levels of donor recognition.

Why a Gift Table Is Useful

It is useful for campaign leaders to know in advance the size of gifts, and the number of gifts at each level, that are likely to be needed to achieve a capital campaign goal. For this reason, a feasibility study report usually includes such a projection in the form of a table of gifts or a gift range table.

A gift table can focus the attention of the campaign leaders on the order of gifts that will be needed and particularly on the large ones that, as campaign experience shows, must provide the lion's share of the total goal.

It can also be used strategically with advance and major gift prospects (who often include campaign leaders) to infer the level of gifts needed from them.

By the mid-1940s, gift tables were constructed in accordance with the "rule of thirds"—a formula that was based on what then was perceived to be generally applicable campaign experience.

According to this "rule," about 10 donors account for the first third of the campaign goal; about 100 donors provide the next third; and all the remaining donors in the constituency furnish the final third.

This formula is flexible only to the extent that any failure in achieving the objective of the top third can be compensated for by exceeding the objective of the middle third; the bottom third, however, cannot make up for any failure in the top or middle thirds.

What a Volunteer Leader Should Know About

Over the past few decades, there has been a departure from the inflexibility of the "rule of thirds" and the development of what could be termed the "specific situation formula" which focuses on the individual organization and the actual potential of its prospects (mainly its prospects for the largest gifts). This focus assumes special importance for organizations with inadequate giving potential below the advance and major gift levels.

How this "specific situation formula" is applied probably can best be shown by taking, as an example, a proposed capital campaign for $4,000,000 by an organization which (a feasibility study disclosed) has three advance gift prospects capable of and interested in making gifts totaling $2,000,000.

For a $4,000,000 campaign goal, these three potential gifts (one for $1,000,000 and two for $500,000 each) are much larger than any gifts that would ordinarily be included in a gift table based on the "rule of thirds"; the usual lead gift in such a table would be $400,000 or 10 percent of the goal.

With the "specific situation formula," however, the three potential gifts totaling $2,000,000 are included in the gift table. Indeed, if these gifts were not shown to be needed by the gift table, the prospects capable of giving them would probably make much smaller gifts.

This example is illustrated further in Appendix I, which shows two gift tables. The one titled "$4 Million Goal Based on Rule of Thirds" arranges the size of gifts, and the number needed at each level, according to its formula. The other one titled, "$4 Million Goal Based on Specific Situation Formula," includes the three unusually large gifts.

The "Rule of Thirds" gift table shows the top nine donors accounting for a total of $1,400,000—or 35 percent (just over a third) of the campaign goal. The "Specific Situation Formula" gift table shows the top seven donors providing a total of $2,400,000—or 60 percent (nearly two-thirds) of the campaign goal.

What the Board Should Give

There is no simple rule that can be generally applied. A third of a

FUND RAISING IN GENERAL

campaign goal provided by board members could be generous for one organization's campaign and inadequate for another's. The same could be true of a fifth or a tenth of a campaign goal.

Every campaign requires a separate determination, which should be aided by the feasibility study's analysis and recommendation on what board members as a whole could pledge.

Board members should pledge generously and in proportion to their individual means and to the amount of the goal. With such pledges, they would demonstrate their enthusiastic support of the campaign and set the example for all other prospective donors.

The pledges of board members should achieve 100-percent participation, as well as reflect proportional giving. Prospective donors could well want to know—and would have every right to ask—what the board as a whole has pledged and whether all board members have participated.

What a board as a whole should give, then, is the total of the estimates of what all members could give if they pledged generously in proportion to their individual means. A total estimate provided by a feasibility study report should not be taken as final.

A few board leaders usually undertake to solicit the other board members because they would be influential with them, and these leaders are the ones who know the board members best and can most accurately estimate their giving capacity. Their estimate of the total board potential could be higher than that which a study indicates because the study reflects the board member's initial giving intentions and not necessarily what they would pledge after a campaign was enthusiastically adopted and after they were effectively solicited.

Another factor is important in determining the portion of a campaign goal the board should—or should try to—provide: the portion of the goal that can realistically be expected to be furnished by all other potential contributors. Where the board represents most of the prospects for substantial support, its share of the goal may necessarily have to be large; where the board represents less of these prospects, its share of the goal can be proportionately smaller.

The determination of a board's share of the campaign goal should therefore be based on an evaluation of its total giving potential and an estimate of what it has to furnish to make up the difference between what all other prospective donors are likely to give and the total goal.

What a Volunteer Leader Should Know About

How a Nucleus Fund Is Formed

A nucleus fund represents the total pledges needed from advance gift prospects, who include mainly the members of the board and any other prospects who in advance or at the outset of a campaign could be capable and ready to make very substantial pledges.

The initial pledges from board members could include large pledges and modest ones, since their giving potential would vary; the commitments from the other advance gift prospects should be among the largest pledges the campaign could attract. Thus, the nucleus fund would demonstrate the support of initial donors for the campaign's objectives; and get it off to an auspicious start that could encourage other prospects, when called on, to pledge generously.

The same few influential board members who solicit their fellow members could complete the nucleus fund by also soliciting the other advance gift prospects. A nucleus fund could be sufficiently large (perhaps as much as a third of the campaign goal) to enable an organization to issue a public announcement of a campaign (which is usually scheduled when an impressive share of the goal is achieved to indicate that the campaign is off to a successful start).

How Major Prospects Can Be Involved

Prospective major donors who are appropriately involved in the affairs of an organization can be expected to lend generous support to a capital campaign. While some prospects may have their own reasons for not wanting to be involved, most prospects welcome the opportunity to participate in ways which are satisfying or comfortable for them.

Membership on an organization's board is the highest level of involvement, and it can make a very important difference in terms of campaign support. For example, an individual of means who might otherwise contribute $10,000 to a capital campaign could be moved, as a board member, to pledge $100,000.

But every major prospect cannot be on the board. An organization should therefore make full use of its standing and ad hoc committees

FUND RAISING IN GENERAL

to involve such prospects, making sure in every instance that the work of the committee is of interest to the prospect.

Other committees and entities can be formed which can do useful work and provide opportunities for major prospects to participate purposefully. For example, Harvard University's Visiting Committees have enabled its departments, graduate schools, and other separate entities to involve individuals whose advice and support have proved of great value.

Organizations can also establish such other entities as an auxiliary board or a board of counselors, which could have useful purposes and which would include individuals who through their service and support could eventually qualify for the board.

Why a Planned Giving Program Is Important

If your organization has not yet undertaken a planned giving program, it probably recognizes an obligation to consider such a program even though it may be pursuing other fund-raising efforts, including an annual giving campaign and a capital-funds campaign.

It could be interested in exploring the advisability of embarking upon a planned giving program because of these reasons:
1. To develop substantial gifts from individuals within an organization's constituency who otherwise are not capable of giving substantially to a capital campaign or even to an annual giving campaign;
2. To enable prospective donors within the constituency to make more meaningful commitments to a capital campaign by permitting them to make planned gifts in addition to "up-front" gifts of currently available cash or securities;
3. To attract substantial gifts from individuals outside an organization's constituency who are mainly interested in the tax advantages of planned gifts; and
4. To provide for gift support in the future when the organization will probably need even greater income from contributions than it currently requires.

A planned giving program should augment, not detract from, an organization's other fund-raising efforts. Indeed, a planned gift should supplement available resources in enabling a donor to pledge at his best. And a bequest can serve to perpetuate a donor's lifetime annual support, and can be used to build an organization's endowment.

In considering a planned giving program, an organization should recognize these minimum requirements:
1. The board will have to make a genuine commitment to support and help advance the program;
2. A board committee on planned giving will have to be designated;
3. The part-time services of a competent consultant will be needed to provide the planning and overall strategy of the program; and
4. A member of the organization's development department, one who has the interest and flair for this fund-raising specialty, will be required to furnish the day-to-day management of the program (often under the supervision of a consultant).

How To Relate To Your Director of Development

Your organization's director of development (who could also be titled director of fund-raising or support activities) should have the full confidence of volunteer leadership; if he does not deserve that confidence, he should be replaced.

If the director of development merits and enjoys that confidence, he should be accepted as a trusted and essential member of your organization's top volunteer-professional leadership. As such, he should be invited to attend meetings of the board (except, of course, when the board goes into executive session to consider such matters as salaries of the professional staff).

His attendance at board meetings is desirable not just to show his acceptance, though that is not unimportant. It is important to the proper fulfillment of his responsibilities that he be present when matters affecting the organization and its financial welfare are discussed and acted upon. And being present, he can provide whatever advice and guidance the board should want from him before it takes final action on development concerns.

FUND RAISING IN GENERAL

This matter of board attendance is underscored here because so many organizations pursue the policy that a director of development should not be present and should not be privy to the board's private deliberations. Aside from being unwise, this policy is a delusion. There are few—if any—such organizations in which the lowest-ranking staff member does not know practically all the board's so-called secrets.

It is vitally important that a development director have free and direct access to board members. Some organizations require him to go through the executive director. Yet his work requires direct access to board members whose knowledge, advice, and assistance he may need on any number of occasions; and indirect access to them loses much in the process both in terms of time and substance. Besides, a development director is like everyone else: he responds and produces most effectively under conditions of mutual respect and trust.

A development director who merits the trust of his volunteer leadership takes his responsibilities with the greatest seriousness. And he should: his performance rests on his efforts, which are usually measurable by what they produce. His position, then, is always on the line—and with it, his reputation, which is crucially important to his continued employment in the fund-raising field.

How To Relate To Fund-Raising Counsel

Fund-raising counsel may be engaged by your organization to advise on a capital campaign, an annual giving campaign, or any other development activity for which experienced and objective guidance could be needed or advisable. He could be an independent consultant or a senior member of a fund-raising counseling firm.

Obviously, for such a consultant to function effectively, he must merit and enjoy the same trust and acceptance accorded your organization's development director. Indeed, in some instances involving the greatest discretion, he should be one of the very few to be confided in and consulted on matters affecting the organization's financial development.

The main values he holds for an organization are his broad fund-raising experience (usually with somewhat similar organizations), his

What a Volunteer Leader Should Know About

objectivity (which a staff member could not be expected to have), and his independence (his income is derived from a number of organizations and is not dependent on any one).

These values place him in the unique position of being able to "talk straight" to volunteer leaders and, when the occasion demands, give them the plain unvarnished truth.

A recent example comes to mind. A consultant, meeting with members of an organization's board, said to them: "I know your immediate reaction will be adverse, but I believe you should start thinking about an important change in policy that eventually you may have to make." He then described the suggested policy change—and, as he predicted, they were all opposed to it.

After the meeting, however, the president of the organization took the consultant aside and said, "Don't let us discourage you. Keep telling us what we have to hear."

The indispensable consultant is one who considers himself expendable—in the sense that he "calls the shots as he sees them," which could result in the termination of his contract. In many organizations, practically no one else (including board members) seems to have the courage to speak out boldly and face whatever risks that may entail.

How To View Fund-Raising Costs

Sooner or later, as a volunteer leader, you will be concerned with fund-raising costs and will find it helpful to have a point of view about them. Even if your organization's costs are not excessive you will find that questions will be raised by donors and prospects—and often for no reason other than their own information.

What fund-raising costs should be in general is a subject of continuing national debate which, as you have probably observed, often generates more heat than enlightenment.

The United Way can operate with low fund-raising costs because it makes only one appeal annually to the business community on behalf of a considerable number of charitable causes; it solicits contributions from corporations and gifts from employees at their places of work (mainly through an economical and relatively painless payroll deduc-

FUND RAISING IN GENERAL

tion plan). Organizations which do not participate in a federated campaign are likely to experience more difficulty and higher costs in raising funds because they do not enjoy the advantages of federated fund raising.

An organization concerned with cancer or heart disease certainly has a stronger and more emotional appeal than an agency devoted to a disease which is less well known and less likely to elicit as strong an emotional response. Therefore, an organization concerned with cancer or heart disease should be able to raise funds more economically. Yet any other agency, whatever the legitimate health cause it espouses, has the same right in our free society to advance its cause even though it incurs higher fund-raising costs.

A prestigious Eastern preparatory school could spend less than 5 percent on fund raising if its constituency has been cultivated over the years and if its campaign objectives are sound and attractive. A newly established secondary school in Appalachia, however, might have to spend even 90 percent on fund raising initially to gain a body of supporters because it has no recourse other than to buy, from list brokers, thousands of names of donors to somewhat similar causes and to undertake broad-scale appeal mailings.

Fund-raising costs alone, then, are not a satisfactory yardstick for determining whether an organization merits financial support. An organization with high costs may provide very valuable services, and an agency with low costs may furnish services of doubtful value.

The development of your own point of view about fund-raising costs will be useful to you in dealing with any specific problems that may arise within your own organization, as well as in countering any criticisms based on the simplistic position that fund-raising costs alone provide a measure of the worth of your (or any) organization's services.

What To Know About State Regulation of Charities

It is important for you to know whether your state regulates the solicitation of charitable contributions; and if it does, what the regulations are and what your organization must do to comply with them.

FUND RAISING IN GENERAL

Since 34 states had (as of December 1981) enacted legislation governing charitable solicitation and administration, the likelihood is that your state is among them.

The Philanthropy Monthly maintains a comprehensive directory of state regulations affecting charitable contributions. The American Association of Fund-Raising Counsel, which is working for uniformity in the regulations (which vary from state to state), annually issues a Compilation of State Laws Regulating Charities which indicates the extent of each state's requirements.

The compilation shows, to cite one example, that Connecticut requires a charitable organization to register with the Assistant Attorney General; limit fund-raising costs to 25 percent to 50 percent, depending on the total raised; make an annual financial report within five months of the close of the fiscal year; and be audited by an independent accountant if contributions exceed $25,000. The state's monetary exemption ceiling is $5,000.

While Connecticut requires no charitable solicitation disclosure, 17 other states have such a requirement (Kentucky, for example, requires that the registration receipt be shown to the donor). Connecticut is one of 24 states which now sets limitations on fund-raising costs.

4

What a Volunteer Should Know About

Recent Fund-Raising Trends

Why a Knowledge of Trends Is Important

There are two reasons why it is important for you to know the trends in fund raising that have developed in the past 10 to 20 years. This knowledge will increase your understanding of how fund raising is practiced today, and it will furnish you with clues to the trends that are likely to develop in the next decade.

Some of the trends noted here evolved in recent years; some surfaced as early as 20 years ago. The past two decades, however, provide an adequate time span for considering the totality of these trends.

Government Increased Its Support of Charitable Causes

The major trend was the increased level of government support of philanthropic causes. In 1974, it was estimated that private giving in the United States was $25.6 billion and that government support totaled $23.2 billion. Thus, by that year, government had become virtually an equal partner with philanthropy—in the work of philanthropy!

This major trend was accompanied by related trends, which helped account for the fact that government support of educational, health, welfare, civic, and cultural causes was widely acceptable and accepted —and, indeed, aggressively cultivated.

The Attitude Changed Toward Government Support

In past decades, the conservative leaders of nonprofit institutions tried their best to avoid government subvention, which they believed carried with it the threat of government control; and conservative donors often contributed heavily to help avert this danger. This attitude changed significantly, and many leaders who once feared government support became active solicitors of public funds for their philanthropic causes. At least partially responsible for this change in attitude was the fact that, as government support increased, the threat of government control did not materialize.

The Need for Government Funds Increased

Probably the main reason for the increase in government support— and for its general acceptance by the public—was the broader recognition that greater government support was required because of the growing financial needs of charitable organizations and because philanthropic funds did not increase proportionately to meet them.

Support and Tax Incentives Were Then Reduced

Financial conservatism became evident in the federal and state governments in the late 1970s. And in 1981 the federal government, concerned with balancing the budget, made substantial cutbacks in support and called on the private sector to compensate for the reductions. Ironically, the Economic Recovery Tax Act of 1981 had the effect of lessening tax incentives for philanthropic giving.

RECENT FUND-RAISING TRENDS

Tax-Supported Institutions Received Private Support

Tax-supported and tax-assisted educational institutions required private funds for needs for which tax dollars were not adequate or allocable. Therefore, at least until 1981, while there was more government support of privately supported universities, there was also more private support of tax-supported and tax-assisted educational institutions.

State Regulation of Gift Solicitation Increased

State regulation of the solicitation of charitable contributions became a fact of life, if not a concern, for most organizations. The number of state governments which directly regulate solicitation increased in recent years from 15 to 34. There was a correspondingly large increase in the number of changes that were made in existing statutes.

The reasons that were attributed to this growing interest on the part of legislators ranged from the desire to protect the giving public from an occasional unethically administered charitable organization to the belief that a legislator could make political capital with such a concern.

Moved by occasional abuses and misrepresentations by some charitable organizations, intermittent attempts were made in the 1970s to enact stronger federal regulation of charitable solicitation; none of them had succeeded by the end of the decade. In late 1979, Carl Bakal, a writer and social critic, called for a new federal agency that would oversee charities and take action against abuses, a number of which he recounted in his book, *Charity USA*.

An article urging such a federal agency appeared over Mr. Bakal's signature in the New York *Times* of October 25, 1979. This proposal was vigorously opposed by John W. Gardner, former Secretary of Health, Education and Welfare, who then headed Common Cause. A letter from Mr. Gardner appeared in the New York *Times* of November 8, 1979, under the heading, "Don't Mess With Our Country's Charities." It is presented as Appendix J because it makes an eloquent case for the continuation of the relative freedom of the nonprofit or voluntary sector from federal intrusion.

Private Organizations Studying Fund-Raising Costs

Government's increasing concern over fund-raising costs was shared by private organizations engaged in philanthropic activities. In recent years, a cost study was initiated by the National Society of Fund-Raising Executives, with the participation of such other agencies as the Council of Better Business Bureaus, the National Information Bureau, the American Association of Fund-Raising Counsel, the National Health Council, and the American Institute of Certified Public Accountants.

The study's objective was to develop bases for determining "reasonable costs" that would satisfy the interests of both donors and charitable organizations. The results, as expected, showed that "reasonable costs" vary considerably for different types of fund-raising activities (such as annual direct-mail appeals, capital campaigns, and long-term planned giving programs); and that there is no validity to the simplistic tendency of taking the "bottom line" percentage of costs as a fair measure of the effectiveness and efficiency of a charity's operations.

Competition for the Donor's Dollar Intensified

There was increasing competition for the charitable dollar because the needs of charitable organizations rose sharply and because the number of such organizations proliferated in recent years. Consequently, there was a greater need for organizations to make a strong case for support (by critically evaluating programs and avoiding duplication of the efforts of other agencies), to attract effective leaders and dedicated workers, to improve fund-raising techniques, and to make their cause heard above the general din.

RECENT FUND-RAISING TRENDS

Charitable Appeals Proliferated

The giving public in recent years was somewhat overwhelmed by the proliferation of appeals to which it was subjected. One effect of this situation was to confuse prospective donors about the priorities of need, since practically all appeals were "urgent." Another effect was to make potential donors callous, as they realized that they could not give to all—or even a fair number—of the appeals.

United Way Movement Was Strengthened

The multiplicity of charitable appeals in cities throughout the country strengthened local United Ways, which continued to represent a problem for organizations campaigning for support independently.

Organizations Needed More Funds Annually

Virtually every charitable organization recognized that it needed more funds annually to remain viable and relevant. Due to rising costs alone, organizations needed constantly increasing annual funds "just to stand still" and not lose ground. Cutbacks in federal support and reduced tax incentives for donors added to organizations' financial problems.

Foundation Payout Requirements Kept Changing

In recent years, the payout requirements for foundations were twice changed by the federal government. The Tax Reform Act of 1969 made it necessary for a foundation to distribute all of its adjusted net income annually; and if in any one year the net income was not equal to 5 percent of the foundation's noncharitable assets, a portion of the foundation's principal had to be combined with its income to meet this 5 percent requirement.

Under the Economic Recovery Tax Act of 1981, however, a foundation does not have to distribute more than 5 percent of its assets. With this change, any investment return above the payout requirement can be used by a foundation to build its assets.

Joint Foundation-Corporation Funding Developed

Some corporations worked with foundations to provide joint funding for such social programs as rehabilitating run-down housing in locations from Bedford-Stuyvesant in Brooklyn to Watts in Los Angeles.

The Ford Foundation, for example, helped create Neighborhood Housing Services, a nationwide program of public and private investment in older sections of 54 cities, which rehabilitated more than 2,500 units with loans totaling in excess of $19 million. The Equitable Life Assurance Society of the United States loaned the program $1 million to help rehabilitate additional units.

The William Penn Foundation was assisted by 22 commercial banks and savings and loan associations in the Philadelphia area in establishing a program for high-risk home rehabilitation loans.

Foundations Funded Development Programs

A number of foundations made grants to strengthen the fund-raising capabilities of organizations and institutions in which they were interested. This was the purpose of an Andrew W. Mellon Foundation grant for the National Audubon Society's development department.

The Ford Foundation made grants for this same purpose to a number of predominantly black colleges in the South and even engaged the services of a fund-raising counseling firm to provide on-the-scene guidance and supervision.

The Ford Foundation also sponsored a program to train black fund raisers for the predominantly black colleges. Trainees proposed

RECENT FUND-RAISING TRENDS

by the presidents of these colleges were given on-the-job experience as interns at a number of the more effective Eastern college development offices.

In spirit, these grants represented a logical extension of the challenge grants which so many foundations made to encourage the recipients of their funds to raise additionally needed financial support.

Corporations Gave Far Less Than the Law Allowed

Corporations were permitted by the 1981 tax law to make charitable contributions totaling 10 percent of their pre-tax net income. Previously, while they were allowed to give up to 5 percent, most corporations gave little more than 1 percent. In 1976, 23 corporations in Minneapolis joined in the common purpose of giving at least 5 percent; their numbers increased to 45 in mid-1981. And by then, "5 percent clubs" had formed in Baltimore and Louisville; and were being formed in Dallas, Denver, Detroit, Jacksonville, and Oakland.

Corporate Support of the Arts Became Fashionable

Many corporations appreciated that support of the arts was good for business. They gave to the arts in the recognition that they could derive a good return in terms of both advertising and public relations. Indeed, they often found that the return was far better than they could gain from corresponding expenditures in "straight" advertising. Businesses also began buying and showing art on their premises; and this trend was strengthened by the growing awareness that good art represents an investment that appreciates more—and more reliably—than many a blue-chip stock.

Campaign Leaders Were in Short Supply

Volunteer leaders with the capability and experience of heading major capital campaigns became increasingly overcommitted or otherwise unavailable; and there was at least the impression that, with important exceptions, the next generation of available campaign leaders was not sufficiently numerous or influential. This impression was probably due to such factors as the larger number of institutions that undertook major campaigns, the great increase in the amount of campaign goals, and the memory (however accurate) of philanthropic leaders of previous years.

Volunteer Leaders Knew More About Fund Raising

Overall, however, volunteer leaders were far better informed on fund-raising concepts and practices than many of their predecessors. The reasons were obvious: fund-raising knowledge continued to expand, and more volunteer leaders were exposed to it. And this increased knowledge paid off in increased fund-raising returns.

Patterns of Volunteer Service Changed

Volunteering for philanthropic causes, which was once the special preserve of the social elite, became for others with social aspirations a well-traveled avenue of social acceptance. Men, as well as women, took this route.

For the upper and middle economic classes in general, however, philanthropy was an accepted way of life. The pattern for women was going to college, getting married, settling down, and becoming a volunteer. For men, the pattern was going to college, starting a career, and volunteering when work permitted (at night and briefly during the day).

As the 1970s came to a close, the pattern for women changed markedly. More and more women started to work for pay (because they needed the money or wanted to pursue careers) and were unavailable during working hours. Since women constituted by far the largest part of the volunteer force, many gift-supported organiza-

RECENT FUND-RAISING TRENDS

tions heavily dependent on volunteer service were hard hit by this development, and began to explore ways of adjusting to it.

More Organizations Engaged Professional Fund Raisers

There was more reliance on professional fund raisers than ever before. Practically every institution or organization of even modest size engaged a staff fund raiser and/or a consultant as they realized that they would need increasingly greater funds every year and that raising such funds required professional direction.

The Professional Fund Raiser Started To Lose His Anonymity

In previous years, the professional fund raiser was an almost unseen presence lurking in the background, conferring privately with volunteer leadership, and transmitting his advice indirectly through others. This started to change; and fund raisers more often spoke directly to board members and campaign leaders, occasionally assisted in presentations to prospective donors, and (when the situation required it) even addressed direct appeals to prospects.

Capital Campaigns Set Astronomical Goals

Some large institutions—mainly universities—set dollar goals in the hundreds of millions—goals which no longer represented just needs but (as fund-raising consultant Robert L. Conway, of Brakeley, John Price Jones Inc., viewed them) "needs plus aspiration plus mission or sense of destiny." These goals were unattainable in the usual capital campaign period of two or three years. As a result, campaigns for such goals extended to five or more years. Not all of these campaigns succeeded; and some of those which achieved their goals resorted to such "bookkeeping" devices as counting gifts toward a goal which were not given directly to the campaign or not contributed during the campaign period.

Capital Campaigns Raised More Funds in Less Time

In general, capital campaigns became comparatively shorter. Previously, a capital campaign was usually phased, with immediate objectives to be completed in about two years, and longer-range objectives to be achieved over the balance of the decade. This changed, and goals that formerly would have been spread over 10 years were often attempted in two or three years. Thus, even those campaigns which needed several more years were achieved in half the time they would have previously required.

Capital Campaigns Were Needed More Frequently

Capital campaigns once every decade may have been adequate in the past, but institutions began to recognize that capital needs were being identified—and had to be met—more frequently. As a consequence, some institutions started capital campaigns almost as soon as the pledges to previous campaigns were paid. And other institutions inaugurated long-term capital development programs which extended up to 10 years and consisted of a series of phases, with the goal of each phase capable of being enlarged as additional capital needs were identified.

Capital Campaign Timetables Became More Flexible

The fund-raising principle evolved that a capital campaign should be free of any undue concern with the calendar or a predetermined timetable, and should proceed on the basis of a sequence of solicitations, starting with the most important and taking whatever time is needed to complete them before embarking upon the next most

RECENT FUND-RAISING TRENDS

important solicitations. This principle grew out of a recognition that solicitation for the important commitments should not be rushed, that donors have their own schedules of when they want to give, and that adjusting to their notions makes good campaign sense.

Larger Gifts Comprise Greater Shares of Campaign Goals

Even in previous years, the larger gifts usually accounted for about 66 percent of a capital campaign goal; in recent years, however, these gifts often represented as much as 85 to 90 percent. This increase was probably due to greater concentration on major gift prospects and more effective solicitation.

Smaller Gifts Were Diverted to Annual Giving

As the larger gifts assumed greater importance in a capital campaign, some institutions took the position that all members of their constituencies should not be asked for capital commitments; and that the rank and file, capable of only modest capital commitments, should be encouraged instead to contribute at their best to annual giving—and then to perpetuate their lifetime giving through bequests. This position was contrary to previous thinking: that every member of a constituency should—and had a right to—be asked to contribute to a capital campaign.

Capital Campaigns Stressed Education and Cultivation

There was greater awareness of the vital importance of careful education and cultivation of major gift prospects before they were solicited. Such prospects were viewed as too important to be rushed into commitments before they were prepared to pledge at their best, since their gifts comprised the lion's share of a capital campaign goal. Solicitors were therefore asked to make more than one call on their prospects even when the time for solicitation was appropriate—to explore with the prospects how they could make the most generous commitments their financial situations permitted and to enable their prospects to consult with their families and tax consultants.

Funds Were Borrowed for Construction and Raised Later

With sharply rising building costs, there was a growing tendency before the late 1970s to borrow funds for construction (so building could be started at once) and then to raise the funds to repay the loans, which frequently came from government, both federal and state. It was not unusual for an institution to borrow the funds it needed, rather than to invade its endowment; and to invest its endowment funds aggressively so as to be able, it hoped, to show a profit after repaying the loan.

Income-Producing Potential of Frozen Assets Developed

A few institutions that owned valuable land which had not been developed to the full extent permitted by local zoning undertook programs that enabled them to realize the income-producing potential of their frozen assets. Here are examples of two institutions that profited substantially from such development programs.

The Friends Select School in Philadelphia, standing on land deeded to it by William Penn and located in an area which had become a business district, was a privately supported secondary school with outdated facilities, limited operating funds, and meager sources for needed additional support.

It interested a major corporation in taking a 99-year lease on its valuable property and constructing a 20-story office building through an arrangement which made it possible for Friends Select to erect a new school building and eventually to receive annual income for its maintenance.

The Museum of Modern Art in New York City needed greatly

RECENT FUND-RAISING TRENDS

increased endowment, additional earned income, renovation and modernization of its building, and a new wing to double its gallery space. It undertook a program that combined a $75 million capital campaign with the development of the income-producing potential of its air rights.

The Trust for Cultural Resources, a public benefit corporation created by the state legislature, provided the financing (through a $40 million bond issue) for the six-story wing and the Museum's renovation and modernization; and arranged for the sale of the Museum's air rights to a developer for the construction of a commercially financed 44-story condominium tower above the wing.

From this complex program, the Museum will gain these benefits: an improved and enlarged building; additional endowment of $75 million (including $17 million for the sale of the Museum's air rights); greater annual income from increased memberships which the larger Museum will accommodate; greater earned income from increased admissions and sales of auxiliary services; and additional annual income of $3 million from condominium owners' tax equivalency payments when the bond debt and other Trust obligations are met.

Capital Campaign Payments Level Continued for Annual Giving

Some donors to capital campaigns, after they completed the annual payments on their pledges, tended in subsequent years to continue to contribute at the same level to annual giving. They helped make it possible for a number of the leading universities to receive gifts totaling up to $25 million or more a year during periods when capital campaigns were not undertaken.

Annual Giving Attracted Larger Gifts

As their fund-raising techniques improved, annual giving campaigns started to attract bigger gifts, some of which were as large as

$10,000 to $25,000—amounts which only a few years before were considered capital commitments.

Annual Giving Was Seen as Substitute for Endowment Income

For many institutions which needed far greater endowment funds, additional endowment proved hard to come by. This was particularly true of unrestricted endowment, their most urgent need, because such gifts were not attractive to prospective donors. Indeed, many prospective donors indicated they would rather invest their funds and donate the income. This experience led a few institutions to the realization that annual giving could be aggressively developed to provide the annual equivalent of income from endowment.

Some Endowment Funds Were Invested for Greater Return

Some institutions in the late 1960s and early 1970s adopted a new policy toward the investment of their endowment funds that took capital gains, as well as dividends and interest, into account in investing for the highest overall return. They therefore invested more heavily in stocks which, though their dividends were low, had high-growth potential. And they figured that if the return should prove inadequate for their needs, the difference between that return and what it would have been under a more conservative policy could be obtained by using part of the capital gains. In the years that followed, however, stock market behavior adversely affected this innovative policy, and substantial losses were sustained.

Health Education Was Coupled with Fund Raising

The major national voluntary health organizations combined their fund-raising activities with educating the public on the health causes they represented; the funds they raised benefited medical research, as well as public, patient, and professional education.

RECENT FUND-RAISING TRENDS

The American Cancer Society, which raises more funds annually than other national voluntary health organizations, armed its over 1.6 million door-to-door volunteer solicitors with 50 million educational leaflets for distribution to 40 million households. In 1981, the Society raised over $165 million—a striking example of how education leads to understanding and then to support.

Public Television Became Another Charitable Cause

Public television stations during the past two decades joined the long list of causes seeking contributions from the public. During that period, they first raised operating support through memberships and annual gifts; then, with the encouragement of matching challenge grants offered by The Ford Foundation, a number of them undertook capital funds campaigns.

The fund-raising potential of public television was dramatically demonstrated by WNET/Channel 13, headquartered in New York City, which received the largest Ford Foundation grant ($10 million —to be matched on a dollar-to-dollar basis).

By the end of a five-year campaign, it had raised $13.5 million in capital funds, exceeding its original goal by $3.5 million. During the same period, it also doubled its annual support (dues and gifts) from individuals to $8 million a year (increasing its paid memberships from 125,000 to 300,000); and boosted its direct support of specific programs from foundations and corporations to $8 million a year.

Fund-Raising Association Provided Public Services

The American Association of Fund-Raising Counsel's 30 member firms, which are paid for the services they provide to gift-supported organizations, decided that they also wanted to contribute to the cause of philanthropy; they therefore authorized the Association to undertake a program of public service, which set an example for other organizations of professional fund raisers. Two of the Association's services are of particular interest.

What a Volunteer Should Know About

It contributed the services of its president, John J. Schwartz, to raise $2.4 million needed in the mid-1970s to support the work of the Commission on Private Philanthropy and Public Needs, which was launched by John D. Rockefeller 3rd and chaired by John H. Filer. The Commission conducted a full-scale examination of the role of philanthropy in the United States.

The Association subsequently organized, provided initial funding, and still furnishes the major continuing support of a monitoring service that identifies and studies all proposed state legislation seeking to regulate charitable solicitation; and alerts the leading national charitable organizations and groups on pending bills which would adversely affect them.

Fund-Raising Counsel's Role Was Not Always Clear

It was not unusual, even during the 1970s, for the president of an organization undertaking a capital campaign to assume that fund-raising counsel was not needed when a competent director of development was on the staff and providing day-to-day campaign management.

Such a president did not realize that, in a capital campaign for an ambitious goal, the organization could benefit importantly—and gain greater insurance against the risks of such an undertaking—by having the input of both the director of development and fund-raising counsel.

And more than a few directors of development, particularly those serving presidents with this attitude, felt somewhat uncomfortable about requesting or using fund-raising counsel, as if the involvement of counsel would indicate a lack of competence on their part.

Robert P. Roche, who heads the fund-raising counseling firm of Barnes & Roche, Inc., was moved in the late 1960s to confront the basic question of the validity of retaining a fund-raising consultant. "Why a Consultant?", which appears as Appendix K, gives his answer.

RECENT FUND-RAISING TRENDS

A Permanent Commission on Philanthropy Was Created

A new organization, the Independent Sector, was formed in 1980 to serve as the kind of permanent commission on philanthropy that was recommended in 1975 by the Commission on Private Philanthropy and Public Needs.

By the close of 1981, its members included about 350 national non-profit organizations and agencies, and foundations and corporations with national interests. Its membership constituted a merger of the National Council on Philanthropy (donors) and the Coalition of National Voluntary Organizations (donees).

The five-part program of the Independent Sector, as delineated by John W. Gardner, who became the first chairman of its board, has these objectives: "public education to improve understanding of the sector's role and function in giving people alternatives, greater opportunities for participation and for creating a more caring and effective society; communication within the sector so that shared problems and opportunities may be identified and pursued; relationships with government to deal with the infinite interconnections between the two sectors, but particularly to ensure the healthy independence and continued viability of non-governmental organizations; research to provide a body of knowledge about the independent sector and about how to make it most useful to society; and encouragement of effective operation and management of philanthropic and voluntary organizations to maximize their capacity to serve individuals and society."

The Importance of the Computer Was Recognized

The computer was broadly recognized as an important fund-raising tool. Among the ways it helped were: information on prospects was stored and rapidly retrieved in a number of desirable arrangements (such as by age, status, sex, or size of gift); and computerized mailings for certain groups of prospects and donors provided a more effective and economical method of raising funds by mail.

5

What a Volunteer Should Know About

Likely Future Trends

How These Likely Trends Can Be Used

For this forecast of trends likely to develop in the 1980s, the author consulted his own crystal ball. It is really not important whether these trends do—or do not—develop, or whether they come in the 1980s or thereafter. What is important is that the volunteers (the leaders and the solicitors who will become leaders), whose views and actions will actually shape the new trends in fund raising, devote advance thought to what could best provide for the support of the nation's gift-supported organizations. This forecast, to the extent that it helps focus such advance thinking, can serve a useful purpose.

Annual Giving Campaigns Will Become More Effective

Annual giving campaigns will increase in effectiveness as they continue to make wider use of capital campaign techniques (particularly in-person solicitation of prospects capable of giving substantially), to offer gift opportunities to raise annual giving sights, and to set recognition categories for donors at increasingly higher giving levels.

The largest gifts to annual support will come from many of the major donors of institutions which have conducted capital campaigns. As these donors complete the substantial annual payments on their capital campaign pledges (which could have extended over three to five years), some of them will continue to provide the same level of yearly support for subsequent annual giving campaigns.

More Foundations Will Give to Annual Support

Foundations in general will be torn between their traditional preference for funding new programs and a growing awareness of the urgent need for annual operating support by the established institutions. As a result, more foundations will start to make grants for annual support; they will consist mainly of middle-size and small foundations which have more flexibility than the largest foundations because they are not as firmly committed to specific areas of interest and grant-making policies.

Corporations Will Give More for Annual Operations

Corporations will increase their contributions toward the annual operating expenses of charitable organizations, as the concept of corporate citizenship takes firmer hold and they act on the public expectation they will help offset cutbacks in government support.

Arts organizations in particular will receive more—and more substantial—support from corporations, which will be encouraged by major contributions of leading corporations and by the public recognition and approval such gifts engender.

Nontraditional Organizations Will Make Headway

The nontraditional organizations, many of which are activist or advocacy groups, will continue to seek greater financial support; they

LIKELY FUTURE TRENDS

will be aided by the National Committee for Responsive Philanthropy, which will maintain its efforts in their behalf for a larger share of the charitable dollar.

Whether these groups will make appreciable headway will depend upon whether they will undertake to increase their fund-raising ability (such as by strengthening their boards and the case for their support) and by meeting in general the standards required by local United Ways for member agencies.

Intensive Capital Campaigns Will Continue To Be Held

The intensive capital campaign will be undertaken in the future by those institutions for which it represents the most effective and least expensive method of raising capital funds.

Institutions which conducted a number of such campaigns will come to view them as stages in a continuing capital development program, with each stage starting upon the completion of the previous one, with each advanced by a fresh volunteer leadership team committed to a new set of needed objectives, and with each having a goal and a closing deadline.

The type of continuing capital development program with no goal and no timetable will suffer because it will have no sense of urgency to motivate volunteers to expeditious action, and because fund-raising leadership eventually tires and cannot be retained indefinitely.

Capital Campaign Goals Will Become More Realistic

In recent years, capital campaign goals have ballooned to $300 million and more. In the 1980s, goals will become more realistic—at least for a three-year time frame—because they must be credible if effective campaign leaders are to be enlisted and if major prospects are to be expected to give substantially. And if one campaign is to follow another, as stages in a continuing capital development program, each campaign will have to succeed if the following one is to be launched under favorable fund-raising circumstances.

Buildings Will Continue To Be Attractive to Donors

Buildings will continue to hold an attraction for capital campaign donors who can afford to put their names on them. Campaign leaders therefore will not relax their efforts to match their projected edifices with the edifice complexes of prospective donors.

But many prospects capable of contributing substantially toward the cost of projected buildings will start to take a harder look at the need for new construction. As a consequence, more institutions will opt for renovation whenever that represents a suitable alternative functionally and a more economical choice in terms of physical alterations and operating costs.

Endowment Funds Will Be Difficult to Raise

Endowment funds generally will be hard to come by. The campaigns most likely to succeed will be those which focus, or concentrate entirely, on funding gift opportunities—endowing programs and services that are attractive or of particular interest to donors.

Campaigns undertaken for unrestricted endowment—the kind that institutions need the most—will face increasing resistance as donor awareness grows that whatever endowment is raised must eventually prove to be inadequate, since endowment income does not keep pace with rising costs. And this resistance will encourage more donors to act on their preference for giving to other purposes which they find more congenial, creative, or personally satisfying.

Endowment Will Be a Partial or Temporary Solution

The volunteer leadership of many an institution in the past tended to view endowment as a final solution to the problem of annual maintenance. In the 1980s, volunteer leaders generally will perceive that endowment at best is only a temporary solution—until its income is exceeded by rising costs; and is more often just a partial solution—

LIKELY FUTURE TRENDS

since its income meets only part of the total need for annual support. In the 1980s, too, endowment will provide less and less of the operating funds an institution needs.

Annual Giving Will Be Equated with Endowment Income

Many institutions will find it unrealistic to expect to obtain all—or even much—of the additional annual income they need from endowment; they will therefore come to view increased annual giving as the equivalent of—and the practical alternative to—additional endowment income.

They will supplant inadequate endowment income with increased annual giving because annual contributions are more often easier to raise, and because few (if any) institutions realize the full annual giving potential they possess.

More Capital Campaigns Will Seek Planned Gifts

More capital campaigns in the future will seek planned gifts, including bequests and gifts of future interests, because these gifts represent funds that would otherwise probably not be contributed to them and because such gifts will be needed after the capital campaign objectives are met. Campaign leaders will be more inclined to view planned gifts as part of a total commitment (including outright gifts of cash and securities) that donors should be asked to consider in determining how they can make their finest contributions.

Unified Development Programs Will Be Undertaken

More institutions will incorporate the intensive capital campaign in a unified development program which will simultaneously seek annual, capital, and planned gifts. And many philanthropically-minded Americans in the upper and upper-middle income brackets will come to recognize the need for such combined giving for the maintenance, if not the survival, of organizations whose programs and services they endorse.

More Boards Will Add To Their Fund-Raising Strength

As boards come to appreciate their central role in fund raising and as operational costs continue to rise, more boards will move to strengthen their ability to give and get financial support. Their efforts will be rewarded to the extent that they screen prospective board members carefully; advise them in advance of their fund-raising responsibilities; and orient them fully when they are enlisted.

Volunteer Services Will Be Scheduled More Flexibly

Gift-supported organizations will continue to lose women volunteers who previously were available for daytime service but who in the 1980s will take paid employment. This loss will be severe: it has been estimated that by the end of the 1980s, 70 percent of all women between the ages of 25 and 44—or a total of 27 million—will be gainfully employed.

Several other groups will help at least partially to compensate for this loss. More men will become volunteers than ever before; and they will consist mainly of retirees, including those who take early retirement. They will enlist because they will want to keep active and to serve in significant causes. More students, men and women, will view volunteer services as a useful outlet for their altruistic impulses.

Many more corporations will encourage their employees to take part as volunteers in community work, and will offer release time so that their employees can serve during the day. These corporations will find that their productivity will not suffer and will probably even improve.

The organizations which will be most successful in attracting and keeping their volunteers will be those that reexamine their operations

LIKELY FUTURE TRENDS

and adjust their schedules to accommodate volunteers' available time. By adopting a more flexible approach, they will find that they can schedule more activities at night and on weekends; and that they can recruit more effectively by offering prospective volunteers shorter assignments and one-time projects, rather than long-term or continuing responsibilities.

Communications Media Will Play a Larger Role

The potential that the communications media possess for helping to advance charitable causes will be more fully developed. Television, radio, and the print media will assume an increasingly larger role in furthering public recognition of philanthropic needs and in stimulating public response to meet them.

The media will be more useful for annual giving drives than for capital campaigns, since annual giving seeks broader bases of support and since capital fund efforts focus mainly on relatively few prospects for substantial commitments who can usually best be solicited before campaigns are publicly announced.

The Use of the Computer Will Continue To Increase

The use of direct mail for the solicitation of gifts will continue to expand. The reason: direct mail will continue to be the only way that large numbers of donors capable of modest gifts can be solicited, since practically no organization will be able to recruit enough volunteers to solicit them in person.

The use of the computer will also continue to increase—and probably at a more accelerated rate. The reason is that the computer will make it easier and more efficient for organizations to store and retrieve information on their donors, use this information to select prospects for special appeals, personalize printed form letters, and eliminate duplicate names from new donor acquisition lists.

What a Volunteer Should Know About

Government's Role in Philanthropy Will Contract

Support of charitable causes by the federal government, which continued to increase until the late 1970s, will decrease to a substantial degree during the decade of the 1980s: and the private sector will not find it possible to compensate for the deep cutbacks in federal support. Indeed, gift-supported organizations will have their hands full in raising the increasingly larger funds that will be needed just to meet continually rising costs.

State Regulation Will Be Less Onerous

Since oversight of charitable contributions is widely accepted as a state responsibility, virtually all states can be expected to enact regulatory legislation by the end of the decade.

But the trend toward federal deregulation that started in the early 1980s should encourage the great majority of states that regulate the solicitation of charitable contributions to eliminate their more onerous requirements.

Under such regulations, the smaller charitable organization must divert staff from providing services to complying with complex reporting requirements; or engage additional staff, which adds to the fund-raising costs with which the states are concerned.

The extent to which "over regulation" will be curbed will be determined by the effectiveness of organizations' volunteer leadership in bringing their views to the attention of legislators, some of whom have focused on charitable regulation as a means of furthering their public careers.

Organizations Will Become More Financially Conservative

Gift-supported organizations in the 1980s will reflect the financial conservatism of government that emerged in the late 1970s and was strengthened at the start of the new decade.

LIKELY FUTURE TRENDS

Like the country's profit-making organizations which have been geared to an expanding economy, nonprofit organizations in the past have viewed as normal the constant expansion of their services. They considered organizations which did not add services as being in trouble, financially or programmatically.

Adjustment in such thinking in the 1980s will not come easily. When it does come, the policy of privately supported organizations will be that new services will be added only if they are important enough to displace present services; and that all services will be periodically assessed, with only those retained which are deemed to be most needed and relevant.

One result will be that more organizations will decide to limit their roles and provide only those services which they are best qualified to offer. This decision could lead such organizations to eliminate services that duplicate those of other organizations, and to share facilities wherever possible. The overall effect of this development would be that organizations, by concentrating on the services they can do best, would be in a position to make the strongest possible case for financial support to donors and prospects.

Despite this change in thinking, organizations will not be indifferent to any important new human needs that may arise; indeed, it would be unrealistic to assume that Americans could resist their characteristic impulse to respond to the extent they can. Philanthropy will therefore not become static in the decade ahead.

Organizations' Services Will Be Affected

Despite cutbacks in federal support, lessened tax incentives for donors, and inflation, most gift-supported organizations will not be reduced to a marginal level of effectiveness, though many may be crippled and a relatively small number may go out of business.

Where a fatality occurs, the cause will be more a loss of program relevance and renewal than a lack of funds and management. For basically, the life of a voluntary organization is in its vision, not in its finances; and an organization with a perfectly balanced budget can easily die if it loses the spark and spirit that brought it into being.

LIKELY FUTURE TRENDS

Philanthropy Ultimately Will Be Strengthened

While some organizations in the future may disappear and others may diminish in significance, the great majority of them will take whatever actions may be necessary to assure their continued relevance and usefulness, thereby meriting increasing support from the private sector.

The philanthropic impulse is too deep-rooted in Americans to be seriously curbed. The problems that will afflict philanthropy in the 1980s will have no more permanent effect than did the problems that plagued it since Colonial times. And in overcoming them, philanthropy ultimately will be strengthened.

APPENDICES

Appendix A

Why Donors Make Large Gifts

There are more than a few motivations that presumably lead donors to make large gifts to charitable organizations. Here are 10 listed randomly, which are among the more realistic motivations frequently cited—

—To assuage guilt feelings
—To counter public hostility
—To gain public recognition and approval
—To attain social acceptance
—To be remembered by posterity
—To gain a tax advantage
—To invest in a cause of personal importance
—To fulfill an obligation of one's station in the community
—To achieve ego fulfillment
—To make something fair (just, or beautiful)

Appendix B

Guidelines for Mail Appeal

Two factors are of major concern in raising funds by mail appeal.
1. The keen competition for the philanthropic dollar.
2. The ease of rejection of an appeal by mail (via the wastebasket, with no solicitor present to urge reconsideration).

In view of the keen competition and the ease of rejection, it is important to avoid these common errors:
1. *Impersonal approach.* Make sure the signer has some connection with the recipient so that the letter can be a personal one.
2. *Inadequate motivation.* Create recipient motivation that leads from attention to interest and action. The lead of the letter should capture the reader's attention or he may never read beyond it.
3. *Incomplete planning.* Second-rate planning usually guarantees second-rate results. Because pains are not taken in advance, they are usually experienced in the returns. Careful planning can also reduce the costs of the appeal and thus increase the net return.

Here are three popular misconceptions:
1. *An appeal letter should be no longer than one page.* The letter should be long enough to make the case for support. Bruce Barton once wrote a four-page letter for Deerfield Academy, and it was the most successful in the school's history.
2. *Every year's appeal has to be completely different.* André Gide said: "Everything has been said already, but since nobody listens, everything has to be said again." Don't be afraid to repeat or rephrase, though each year's letter should look different in some way than its predecessors.
3. *People won't read anything you send them.* They won't read everything, but they will read selectively—if you interest them.

These three observations about the content of a mail appeal are always important to keep in mind:
1. What is *said* is important.
2. *Who* says it is often more important than what is said.

APPENDICES

3. Dramatize the case. To get attention and interest, the letter should deal immediately with anecdote, fact, and topical reference; generalizations are dull.

Whom should the writer of a mail appeal try to please?

1. *Himself.* If a writer does not satisfy himself, he has little chance of pleasing anyone else. When he has finished a draft, he should be ready to stand behind it—against all critics.
2. The *signer.* The writer's draft should be written with the signer in mind. Very often the signer, a volunteer leader, has ideas which are good or which can be refined or developed for effective use.

Here are 10 principles that apply to a mail-appeal effort:

1. *Personal approach.* The degree to which the appeal appears to be personal and individual is in direct proportion to the attention-getting strength of the letter.
2. *Emotional impulse.* Giving is the result of a rationalized emotional impulse.
3. *Proportionate giving.* Giving should be in proportion to the capacity of the donor and the extent of the need. Without these standards, the dollar volume of giving is always low.
4. *Atmosphere of optimism.* Fund raising is always best in an atmosphere of universality (an indication that all are giving) and optimism (an indication that the objective can be achieved).
5. *Sense of genuine urgency.* People tend to be subject to laws of human inertia. A sense of urgency, along with importance, has the best chance of moving them.
6. *Salesmanship of conviction.* An appeal letter must move the recipient from attention and interest to concern, advocacy, and support. It can do this best if it conveys a very real sense of conviction by the signer.
7. *Character of the cause.* The appeal letter should be in keeping with the character of the cause it advances; it should sound like the signer; and it should be appropriate for the recipient.
8. *Repetition and continuity.* A mail-appeal effort should provide for one or more follow-up letters. It is better to appeal to the same good names three times than to write only once to a list three times as large.
9. *Desired level of giving.* Once a donor starts to give at a certain

level, usually he is not easily or quickly persuaded to raise his giving sights. It is therefore important to obtain the first gift at the desired level.
   10. *Worth, not just need.* Large contributions tend to be given to worthy institutions rather than just to needy causes.

A list of "Don'ts" may be helpful for the writer to keep in mind in drafting an appeal letter:
   1. Don't be obscure, fanciful, or wordy.
   2. Don't be tricky, avant-garde, ponderous, or learned.
   3. Don't oversell.
   4. Don't ordinarily have a professional sign an appeal letter; a professional cannot be as effective as a volunteer.
   5. Don't think that words can make up for a weak case for support.
   6. Don't focus on money that is needed; talk about program, which is the best way to attract support.
   7. Don't use a signer of an appeal that the reader would know could not or would not have signed the letter, even though the signature is made to look real.
   8. Don't emphasize tax deductibility, though it should be mentioned. People don't make gifts only because they are tax deductible; and if they did, they could give to practically any other organization.
   9. Don't accept layout or artwork which does not help readability. Mail appeal is judged by the gifts it attracts, not by the art awards it wins.
   10. Don't forget that in making the case for support the cause should be bigger than the organization that advances it.
   11. Don't let those who must approve the draft of an appeal homogenize its content so that it loses its effectiveness.
   12. Don't be afraid to take a chance and break the rules when it's needed.
   13. Don't expect a letter to be anywhere near as effective as a visit or telephone call.

Here are some tips on the mechanics of a mail-appeal effort:
   1. Develop your own lists of prospects. Beware of renting such lists as "10,000 wealthy widows" or "25,000 yacht owners."

APPENDICES

2. Never use a list that has not been carefully checked for accuracy.
3. Make sure that a signer of an appeal letter addresses each recipient appropriately and signs accordingly.
4. Enclose a leaflet in a mail appeal if it helps dramatize the cause through words and pictures. An annual report, if brief, can be used. A return-addressed envelope, with a short program statement on the inside flap, should be enclosed.
5. Arrange for publicity to break as close as possible to the date the appeal letters will be delivered.
6. Remember that testing is the secret ingredient of successful mail appeals. Until an appeal mailing is tested—to see how it draws—its effectiveness is undetermined. Therefore, records (the maintenance of day-to-day data on responses to mailings) are important.
7. Acknowledgments of gifts and appreciation for them deserve special attention. If gifts are promptly and gratefully acknowledged, donors can more confidently be expected to give again and in greater measure.
8. It is thoughtful, as well as rewarding, to communicate with donors at times other than when they are asked or thanked for their support. They should be kept informed periodically of the programs and services that their generosity helps make possible.
9. The type used in an appeal letter and its enclosures should be sufficiently large so they can be easily read. Prospective donors with the greatest giving capacity often have the weakest eyes; and making them strain will not encourage generous responses.
10. The use of wide margins and short paragraphs also makes for readability.
11. The letterhead, whenever possible, should carry names that mean something in the community. Responsible names beget confidence in a cause.
12. The letterhead of the signer of an appeal letter could often be more effective than the organization's.
13. Multiple or facsimile signatures are often undesirable, as they

can destroy the illusion of personalization and give the impression of a mass mailing.
14. Postage stamps on return envelopes may increase the percentage of returns, but they can be criticized on the grounds of expense.
15. The use of color on letterheads increases expense, but it also usually increases the response. It should be tested.
16. Remit or return gimmicks are frowned on, and often generate more animosity than support.
17. Telephone check-ups with secretaries of important prospects —just to make sure the appeal was received—have frequently been effective.
18. Each complaint an organization receives should be accorded a hearty welcome and prompt personal attention. A complaint could represent a chance to develop a thoughtful supporter.
19. Postscripts have a high attention value.

These suggestions could be important because mail appeal returns are apt to be relatively modest:
1. Weigh the feasibility of taking the top 10 percent of annual donors and enlisting volunteers to solicit them in person. The results should be rewarding.
2. Ask volunteers who sign appeal letters to write 10 genuinely personal appeals.
3. Give the prospective donor a clear idea of the level of giving that, it is hoped, he would consider. He should know, and may like to know—even if he does not decide to give that much.
4. Include in an appeal mailing a list of gift opportunities and a gift amount for each. This is an effective and acceptable way of indicating to donors the levels of gifts that are desired.
5. Indicate the additional funds needed over last year's goal, and the reasons that caused the increase, when requesting donors to upgrade the level of their gifts.

For satisfying results, a mail-appeal effort should combine the highest degree of personalization with a planned and continuous program of cultivation, solicitation, follow-up, acknowledgment, and appreciation.

APPENDICES

Appendix C

Procedure for Making a Foundation Request

Here is a step-by-step procedure that an organization could follow in applying to a foundation for a first-time grant:
1. Research the foundation in *The Foundation Directory* to determine its interest in the project for which a grant is desired; then visit the nearest regional cooperating collection of The Foundation Center (a non-profit organization that maintains reference collections in every state) to note the foundation's current philanthropic interests as indicated by its recent grants.
2. Ask for a meeting (before submitting a written request) with the appropriate foundation official and the institution's representatives (the volunteer and professional best able to make the case for the project) and learn of the precise extent (if any) of the foundation's interest.
3. Phone the foundation (if a meeting cannot be arranged) to ascertain the foundation's interest in the project; ask how it prefers a request to be submitted, to whom it should be addressed, and when to submit it; learn, if possible, the extent of the foundation's interest in the proposed project.
4. Personalize the request to a major foundation (that is, have it individually typed and addressed to the appropriate foundation official).
5. Prepare a brief summary of the written request if it is long and detailed; the summary can be in the form of a covering letter.
6. State the purpose of the request early in the proposal.
7. Describe the project for which a grant is requested.
8. Suggest how the project might fit in with the recent philanthropic interests of the foundation.
9. Ask for the amount needed or desired for the project, or for support to the extent the foundation may be interested in providing.

10. Justify the amount requested and detail it to the extent necessary.
11. Cite the purposes of the proposed project.
12. Outline the benefits or values it should produce; state the importance of the proposed project (its current relevance, significance, urgency, need).
13. Show why the institution is well qualified to undertake such a project and to succeed with it.
14. Indicate the appropriateness of the project for the institution and how it fits in with its total program.
15. Describe how the project has been carefully planned for soundness and effectiveness; and, if pertinent, state by whom it was planned.
16. Include (if relevant) information on the larger program of the institution of which the project may be a part (include the overall budget, and indicate the qualifications of the person responsible for the larger program).
17. Include (or attach) the budget for the project.
18. Specify who will administer the project and state his qualifications (foundations, to a great extent, give to qualified people).
19. Attach (if pertinent) the latest annual report and/or financial statement of the institution.
20. State that the request to the foundation has the full support of the board of directors, the administration, and the professional staff (if any).
21. Have the request signed by the official likely to be most influential with the foundation (chairman of the board or president).
22. Indicate the length of time the project is to run; if it is to run after the period of foundation support, indicate what the institution proposes to do to insure the project's continuing support.
23. Provide proof of the institution's tax exemption, or at least state that it has such exemption.
24. Promise to keep the foundation appropriately informed on the use of any grant it may make.

APPENDICES

Appendix D

The Private Sector and Urban Problems

Here are 10 suggestions on how the private sector could focus more funds and leadership on urban problems:

1. By recognizing that the problems of the inner city are not typical philanthropic causes; they are problems which must be met if our urban society—if, indeed, our whole way of life—is to continue.
2. By according urban problems "crisis" priority.
3. By using urban problems as the measure against which all other needs must be compared in establishing the case for support of other causes.
4. By relating the programs and services of the traditional philanthropic causes to the urban problems.
5. By joining with government in an effective partnership to deal with urban problems—not only by providing a decent measure of financial support but by providing the leadership and genius of American business—to assure that success is achieved.
6. By learning to work in partnership with or helping to develop the leadership of the inner city, and by refusing to become discouraged by the difficulties this may represent.
7. By refusing to use the unrest, the disunity, and even the sporadic violence of the inner city as reasons to "cop out."
8. By listening to our children in becoming attuned to the new situation and the new spirit in the land. (The late Whitney Young, Jr., noted that the children of philanthropists by their behavior are providing an educational service in this area.)
9. By recognizing that backing social reforms and improvements does not have to be any more successful than backing medical research; there may well be a lot of waste in both, but we cannot do without either.

10. By starting to deal with the implications of a totally new situation, in which the residents of the inner city (the deprived) do not ask—they demand—a greater measure of the good life that exists on the outskirts of the inner city; they claim the right to determine the use of funds made available for the inner city; and they recognize no obligation at all to express their appreciation for any assistance rendered.

Three considerations bear on these suggestions:

One is that a wholly new breed of philanthropist may have to be raised up whose motivation for giving will not require the good behavior, gratitude, or even respect of the recipients.

Another is that philanthropy for the inner city, if it is to be significant, will have to be a people's philanthropy—the giving of many millions of dollars annually by increasing millions of people of fairly ordinary means.

The main consideration is a very real reservation as to whether the urban crisis is, indeed, a philanthropic cause. While it certainly affords many opportunities for private philanthropy, in its totality the urban problem does not represent a cause as much as it qualifies as a national disaster.

When Texas, Louisiana, and Oklahoma are swept by the ravages of a tornado, the Red Cross may have a role; but basically government steps in with massive public funds and resources—because, in fact, private agencies cannot provide the necessary response.

The problems of the inner city are the most urgent and explosive aspects of the living conditions of the American people, for we are now mainly an urban society and the inner cities, the cores of our population centers, are rotting.

When we as a nation really decide to declare war on the rotting cores of our cities, massive infusions of government funds will be required to do the job. There is no point in blinking this fact. This does not mean that the private sector should not do all it possibly can; it merely recognizes the dimensions of the undertaking.

Appendix E

A Fair Practice Code

All member firms of the American Association of Fund-Raising Counsel conduct their business in accordance with the Association's Fair Practice Code, which states:
1. Members of the Association are firms whose primary business is providing consulting and management service and raising funds for philanthropic organizations. They will not knowingly be used by an organization to induce philanthropically inclined persons to give their money to unworthy causes.
2. Member firms do business only on the basis of a specified fee, determined prior to the beginning of a client relationship. They will not serve clients on the unprofessional basis of a percentage or commission of the sums raised. Intended services and estimated costs are defined in contractual relationships. Additional services, as required, are furnished by mutual agreement.
3. The executive head of a member organization must demonstrate at least a six-year record of continuous experience as a professional in the fund-raising field. This helps to protect the public from those who enter the profession without sufficient competence, experience, or devotion to ideals of public service.
4. The Association looks with disfavor upon firms which use methods harmful to the public, such as making exaggerated claims of past achievements, guaranteeing results, and promising to raise unobtainable sums.
5. No payment in cash or kind shall be made by a member to an officer, director, trustee, or adviser of a philanthropic agency or institution as compensation for using his influence for the engaging of a member for fund-raising counsel.
6. In fairness to all clients, member firms should charge equitable fees for all services with the exception that initial meetings with prospective clients are not usually construed as services.

Appendix F

Designations of Donor Recognition

The designations customarily used by organizations for categories of donor recognition are benefactor, patron, sponsor, and donor. The terms associate and fellow are also used, sometimes as a substitute for donor. The designation of founder is generally employed when appropriate.

These common designations are preferred by organizations because their wide use has made them generally recognizable by the public, and certainly by donors. Thus, a donor who makes a $1 million gift to an organization would ordinarily prefer to be designated a benefactor because he knows that is what most organizations use for—and most people recognize as—designating the largest contributors.

Occasionally, however, the volunteer leaders of an organization want to explore the possibility of offering new and different designations. The New York Philharmonic, in launching an $18 million endowment campaign in the late 1970s, entertained this possibility.

Among the various possible designations suggested were financiers, sustainers, securitors, underwriters, warrantors, consorts, colleagues, regents, governors, councilors, and impresarios. The Philharmonic decided to stay with the commonly used designations because they were generally recognized.

APPENDICES

Appendix G

Planned Gifts in Capital Campaigns?

What are the potential advantages and possible dangers of a capital campaign policy to accept, solicit, and accord full campaign recognition to donors who make planned gifts (including bequests and gifts of future interests) in addition to any outright gifts they may make of cash, securities, and tangible property and real estate?

This policy represents two basic departures from previous capital campaign practice. One is that an institution would accept legally binding gifts of future interests even though they would probably not be received during the campaign. The other is that an institution would accept the assurances of donors, which are not legally binding, that they had provided for it in their wills. In both instances, the institution would give the donors the same campaign recognition it accords donors of current gifts.

These are the potential advantages of this policy:

1. It would give the solicitor another lever with prospective donors and enable them to make more meaningful gifts than they could if they pledged only what they could give from available cash, securities, or other property. For they would be asked to consider a planned gift as an addition to any outright gift they could make.
2. The planned gift would therefore represent additional funds the institution would not otherwise receive.
3. Some of the planned gifts would come in during the course of the campaign; this would be true of a charitable income trust by which a donor could give the income from capital for 10 or more years. And experience has shown that even a bequest program starts to provide income within a five-year period.
4. As for those planned gifts which are realized after the campaign's close, they will be needed and could be used then, if the past is any guide to the future.

5. And this program of incorporating planned gifts into the capital campaign is probably as effective a way as any to stimulate bequests and planned gifts.
6. It would give an institution the opportunity to go to donors who assured it they had provided for it in their wills, and to indicate to them that, if they wanted to benefit from any immediate income tax advantage, they could make their bequests irrevocable. This would benefit the donor and the institution, which would be assured of the bequest.
7. Finally, this policy would give the institution the assurance that it has gone at least half-way in meeting or adjusting to the needs of its supporters; that it has not neglected any reasonable source of support; and that it has done all that it can do to assure a successful outcome of its capital campaign.

These are the possible dangers of this policy:

1. Since such a bequest is not legally binding, the donor could change his will and take out a bequest to the institution. But if he is given full campaign credit and recognition (such as "benefactor" or "patron"), he would feel a special obligation to keep the institution in his will. And the institution, knowing of his intention, would be alerted to keep the donor cultivated, informed, and interested. While some losses may be experienced, the overall result should be beneficial for the institution—and it would gain far more than it would without this policy.
2. Would acceptance of bequests and planned gifts of future interests give the institution an unrealistic basis of achieving its goal? This could be avoided. The campaign could be pressed forward until pledges of outright gifts total the amount needed. Thus, the bequests and planned gifts could be treated as additional commitments that are not counted toward the goal.
3. This separate bookkeeping could also avoid another possible danger: letting the members of the campaign committees relax their efforts to achieve the full goal in gifts available during the campaign period. The emphasis could still be on obtaining outright gifts that are needed and would be counted toward the goal.
4. Would the receipt of planned gifts place an undue burden on the

APPENDICES

institution? For gifts like trusts which require a fiduciary, the donor could be encouraged to establish a relationship with his own bank or trust company. For donors who want the institution to recommend a fiduciary to manage such a trust, the institution could establish a fiduciary relationship with an appropriate bank or trust company. Thus, there should be no undue burden on the institution.

5. Will campaign solicitors have to be planned giving experts? No. When a prospective donor advises that he cannot give all he would like to give—or what is expected of him—the solicitor could learn the prospect's financial situation and then discuss it with the institution's planned giving expert, who could suggest an appropriate planned gift.

The advantages and possible dangers indicate that an institution undertaking an ambitious capital campaign goal—one which it might not achieve through outright gifts of cash, securities, personal property, and real estate—would benefit from a policy along these lines if its dollar goal does not have to be in hand by a set date:

1. That emphasis throughout the campaign will continue to be placed on obtaining outright gifts of cash, securities, tangible property, and real estate; that planned gifts of future interests will be solicited and accepted from prospective donors who otherwise cannot contribute or make sufficiently meaningful outright gifts; and that total or combined commitments of "up-front" and planned gifts will be accorded full campaign recognition.

2. That the campaign will accord the same full campaign recognition to prospective donors for the full amounts they assure the institution that they have provided for it in their wills.

What Volunteers Should Know for Successful Fund Raising

Appendix H

Capital Campaign Timetable

Year	Month	Advance Gift Phase	Major Gift Phase	Special Gift Phase	General Gift Phase
1981	January				
	February				
	March				
	April				
	May				
	June				
	July				
	August				
	September				
	October				
	November				
	December				
1982	January				
	February				
	March				
	April				
	May				
	June				
	July				
	August				
	September				
	October				
	November				
	December				
1983	January				
	February				
	March				
	April				
	May				
	June				
	July				
	August				
	September				

APPENDICES

This timetable shows acceptable time frames for the four phases of a capital campaign spread over 33 months. Campaign experience indicates that such a timetable should be considered as a pre-campaign projection that should be revised during the campaign to adjust to whatever situations and problems may be encountered.

Flexibility is essential in a capital campaign; and any upcoming phase should be started upon the completion of the previous phase (unless certain overlapping is needed or desired), and not upon any arbitrary timetable that is set at the outset of the campaign.

Explanation:

Crossed lined spaces are periods of initial organizational work when volunteers are enlisted, oriented, and assigned prospects to solicit.

Solid black areas are periods of intense campaign activity when prospects are cultivated and solicited.

Horizontally lined areas are periods of continuing cultivation and solicitation.

Appendix I

Gift Tables

$4 Million Goal Based on "Rule of Thirds"

Number of Gifts	Amount of Gift		Running Total	
1	$400,000	$400,000	$400,000	*Top nine donors give $1,400,000, or 35% (just over a third), of total goal.*
2	200,000	400,000	800,000	
6	100,000	600,000	1,400,000	
8	50,000	400,000	1,800,000	
12	25,000	300,000	2,100,000	
15	15,000	225,000	2,325,000	
40	10,000	400,000	2,725,000	
100	5,000	500,000	3,225,000	
325	1,000	325,000	3,550,000	
600	under 1,000*	450,000	4,000,000	

$4 Million Goal Based on "Specific Situation Formula"

Number of Gifts	Amount of Gift		Running Total	
1	$1,000,000	$1,000,000	$1,000,000	*Top seven donors give $2,400,000, or 60% (nearly two-thirds), of the total goal.*
2	500,000	1,000,000	2,000,000	
4	100,000	400,000	2,400,000	
6	50,000	300,000	2,700,000	
10	25,000	250,000	2,950,000	
15	15,000	225,000	3,175,000	
30	10,000	300,000	3,475,000	
60	5,000	300,000	3,775,000	
300	under 5,000*	225,000	4,000,000	

*At an average gift of $750.

APPENDICES

Appendix J

Letter to the New York Times, Thursday, November 8, 1979

Don't Mess with Our Country's Charities

To the Editor:

Carl Bakal (Op-Ed Oct. 25) called for a new "Federal agency that would oversee charities and take action against abuses." I believe it would be a great mistake to create such an agency.

As one who is identified with openness in all public matters, I can readily agree that there is room for improvement in statutory requirements for disclosure by charitable organizations. But Mr. Bakal's proposed Federal agency deserves a second look.

His assertion that "charity is our only industry that is virtually unregulated" can mislead the reader. We must not yield to the currently popular notion that an activity isn't really "regulated" unless it has its very own regulatory body. If an organization is engaged in fraudulent activities, there are already laws at hand to deal sternly with them—and I'm for that.

Mr. Bakal wants "a limit on the amount of money that charities can spend on fund raising," and I'm fully aware of the abuses that have led him to the suggestion. Unfortunately, it is often the emerging or unpopular organizations which have to spend a lot (relative to the amount taken in) to garner enough funds to pursue their causes. Although the public has a right to know what the costs are, the Government should not have the authority to prohibit those organizations from presenting their case to the public.

But my concern about Mr. Bakal's proposal rests on more fundamental ground. What the public thinks of as "charity" is an inseparable part of our nonprofit, or voluntary, sector. It's no accident that this sector of our national life has so far been relatively free of Federal intrusion. That's the way Americans want it. In the late 17th and early 18th century, British colonial governors new to their posts were often startled by the American habit of solving their problems through voluntary association. And that tradition has produced a nongovernmental, nonprofit sector astonishing in its richness and diversity.

From those early colonial governors down to the present, governing bodies have learned that Americans treasure the freedom of their voluntary sector. It permits citizens to contribute their own time and energy to solve problems they themselves identify. It is a haven for mavericks (liberal and conservative). The sector has been the birthplace of virtually every significant social movement of the past 100 years, from abolitionism to women's rights. The abuses are at most the soiled fringe of a great American tradition. When you go after the abuses, don't mess with the tradition.

If a commission is given the powers that Mr. Bakal proposes, it would have a mighty lever over all kinds of voluntary associations, including those irritating groups that think the Federal establishment could be doing a better job. Indeed, a commission with the powers proposed could smother such critics. All experience tells us that if government has such powers, sooner or later it will use them.

JOHN W. GARDNER
Washington, Oct. 30, 1979

The writer, former Secretary of Health, Education and Welfare, is chairman of Common Cause.

What Volunteers Should Know for Successful Fund Raising

Appendix K

Why a Consultant?

By Robert P. Roche (reprinted by permission of the author)

The validity (or lack of it) of an institution retaining a consultant in the area of fund raising is a question which has deservedly been debated in the past. In these days of tightened budgets and cash flow problems, the question is particularly appropriate. We have been asked by several institutions to summarize our response to this fundamental question.

Perhaps the place to start is with some observations gleaned by members of our firm over many years of experience—both as institutional development officers and as consultants to institutions.

1. The people who retain us seem, most often, to be the very people one might think would have the least need of us. A major part of our work is done with institutions which possess highly sophisticated development staffs and enviable records of success in attracting philanthropic gifts. Whatever it is that people like us to bring to an institution, it seems to be most recognized and valued by people who already are doing the business well.
2. Insecure people and departments generally are not interested in having us around. The development officer whose continued employment and influence depend (in his opinion) on building and maintaining an image of personal infallibility is not likely to invite a consultant within his walls. Presumably the fear of being shown up, or wanting in some respect, outweighs the expectation that something of value might be imparted which would add additional luster to his activities.

There probably are two kinds of reasons why consultants are introduced into institutions (both presuppose institutional commitment to vastly expanded programs):

1. Cases where an experienced and competent development staff exists and where the additional expenditure for consultants simply represents a form of insurance to increase as much as possible the odds in favor of success.
2. Cases where the development staff is not experienced and there

APPENDICES

are actual gaps in know-how and technique to be plugged by the consultant. Here again the insurance factor is also an important one.

Hopefully a consultant brings to the development program of an institution (and to the individuals charged with responsibility for that program) some or all of the following elements:

1. Perspective—the ability, through detachment from the heat and clamor of day-to-day activities in an institution, to view problems and opportunities in a broad way, to express objective judgments which are untrammeled by institutional politics or habit patterns.
2. Creativity—the ability to suggest—on the basis of the particular situation found at a given institution—new and hopefully better ways of meeting old and new problems and capitalizing on opportunities. It should be noted that this goes far beyond the too-frequent practice of carrying around a portfolio of ideas garnered at some institutions and attempting to apply them to the problems of others.
3. Experience—an accumulation of questions, possible answers, ideas, and instincts accumulated over a period of years in institutions which are to varying degrees analogous to the client institution. Quite simply this can come down to the ability to avoid past mistakes.
4. Technique—This is probably the least important part of the service as most development officers either possess or have readily available to them plenty of information on how to structure office procedures, establish and maintain records, etc. However, some overview of systems, based on prior experience, can often be helpful. Also there are well-established methods of getting people to *act* which can be imparted.
5. Comradeship—for lack of a better word this is meant to imply the importance of an institutional development officer having a trusted person who is familiar with the broad outlines of his program with whom to talk things over. In the words of Edgar M. Gemmell, former administrative vice president of Princeton University, "I need to have someone to talk to who understands this business."

The importance of this function is too easily underrated. The

APPENDICES

top person in a development department (whether the department be large or small) is a human engineer of sorts. He must balance the capacities and desires of varied groups of people and effectively bring them to the point of productive action. This can be a lonely business involving a continuing danger of becoming so enmeshed in the complicated network of personal relationships that objectivity may be endangered.

The basic question to which development officers, finance committees, and boards must address themselves is whether or not inputs such as those described above are worth the money they cost. We know of no precise formula which can produce a concise answer to this question. It all depends on the situation at each institution, on the experience, work patterns and desires of the development officer, and—of course—on the competence of the consultant.

One situation frequently experienced is where a development officer who wishes to involve a consultant in his work has developed such a strong relationship with his chief executive and board that these people have total confidence in his capacity to accomplish anything he undertakes—they feel he needs no outside help. The only answer to this problem we have been able to come up with is "if you have all that much confidence in him in so many ways, why do you suddenly withdraw that confidence when he tells you that his own good judgment indicates he wants outside counsel?"

Index

A

Acknowledging gifts, 26, 126
Advocacy groups, 112
American Association of Fund-Raising Counsel, Inc., 10, 72, 73, 92, 96, 107, 108
American Cancer Society, 107
American Institute of Certified Public Accountants, 96
Annual gifts, 13, 103, 105
Annual giving campaigns, 11–37, 103, 111, 115; benefits, 16, 32; board contributions, 15, 16, 21; case statement, 18, 19; compared with capital funds campaigns, 42–44; cultivation, 43, 126; goals, 18–20; increased effectiveness, 68, 69; materials, 18; plan, 16, 21; policies, 19; prospects, 14, 16–29, 31, 32, 35; strategies, 18
Annual report, 18
Apartment house canvasses, 16
Appalachia, 91
Arts, support of, 99, 112

B

Bakal, Carl, 95, 138, 139
Barnes & Roche, Inc., 108
Barton, Bruce, 122
Bedford-Stuyvesant (Brooklyn), 98
Benefactor, 21, 47, 53, 78, 79, 134
Benefits, 16, 32
Bequests, 51, 79, 103, 115, 134
Board of trustees (board of directors), 45, 46, 64, 75–77, 116, 142; committees of, 66; enlarge-

145

ment of, 66, 67, 116; gifts, 84–86, 88, 89; relation to director of development, 88, 89; relation to fund-raising counsel, 89, 90; rotation policy, 66; strengthening of, 64–67
Brakeley, John Price Jones Inc., 101
Budget: campaign, 75; operating, 13, 20, 71
Buildings, 40, 41, 49, 104, 114

C

Campaign assignments, 14, 17, 26
Campaign chairmen, 26, 81, 82, 99, 100; businessmen, 81; lawyers, 81; women, 81
Campaign goals. *See* Annual giving campaigns, goals; Capital funds campaigns, goals
Campaign leaders. *See* campaign chairmen
Campaign timetable, 20, 21, 41, 47, 75, 77, 80, 81, 102, 103, 113, 136
Cancer Care, 22
Capital campaigns. *See* Capital-funds campaigns
Capital funds: how raised, 40–42; why needed, 40
Capital-funds campaigns, 39–61, 71, 72, 102, 103, 115; board gifts, 84–86; case statement, 44, 48, 49, 60; compared with annual giving campaigns, 42–44; construction objectives, 40, 41, 48, 49, 104, 114; endowment objectives, 40, 48; frequency, 102, 113; goals, 41, 42, 44, 46, 50, 57, 58, 68, 76, 77, 101, 113, 135; leadership, 41, 80, 81, 90; materials, 49; nucleus fund, 86; plan, 44, 49, 75; pledges, 47, 49, 53, 55–59, 76, 77, 82; policies, 77–79; prospects, 44, 46, 48–50, 53, 55, 56, 58, 68, 70, 74, 76–78, 80, 86
CARE, 31
Charitable income trusts, 52, 54, 135
Charitable remainder trusts, 52, 54, 79, 135
Charity USA, 95
Children's Hospital Medical Center, The (Boston), 67
Coalition of National Voluntary Organizations, 109
Colleges: predominantly black, 98, 99. *See* Universities Commission on Private Philanthropy and Public Needs, The, 12, 108, 109
Committees. *See* Volunteer Committees
Compilation of State Laws Regulating Charities, 92
Computers, 109, 117
Connecticut, 92
Constituency, 91
Construction objectives: *See* Capital funds campaigns, construction objectives; Building(s)
Contributions: total American, 10

INDEX

Conway, Robert L., 101
Corporate support: by payroll deduction plan, 90, 91; by 26 Minneapolis corporations, 99; of annual operations, 112; of the arts, 99; through employees' services, 116
Council of Better Business Bureaus, 96
Council on Foreign Relations, 71
Cultivation, 43, 56, 126, 134

D

Deerfield Academy, 122
Deferred gifts. *See* Planned gifts
Direct-mail appeal. *See* Mail appeal
Donor, 132
Donor recognition, 18, 21, 22, 47, 53, 78, 79, 132, 133, 135
Donors: motivation, 34, 35, 121; use as solicitors, 82
Door-to-door solicitation, 16, 107

E

Endowment: as a partial solution, 114; difficulty in raising, 114, 115; investment of, 14, 104, 106; quasi-endowment, 40; restricted, 40, 114; unrestricted, 40, 106, 114
Equitable Life Assurance Society of the United States, The, 98

Expendable funds, 40

F

Fair Practice Code, 73, 131
Family foundations, 17
Feasibility study, 44, 45, 47, 74–77, 80; use of, 75, 76; written report, 75, 76, 82
Federated campaign. *See* United Way of America
Filer, John H., 108
Finance (budget) committee, 64
Ford Foundation, The, 98, 107
Foundations: as affected by Tax Reform Act of 1969, 97, 98; funding cooperation with corporations, 98; giving for annual support, 112. *See also* Family foundations
Fresh Air Fund, The, 31
Friends Select School, The, 104
Frozen assets, 104, 105
Fund raisers: black, 98; for predominantly black colleges, 98, 99. *See also* Volunteer solicitors
Fund-raising costs, 27, 28, 61, 90, 91, 96. *See also* Regulation of charities
Fund-raising counseling firms: counseling services, 45, 46, 69, 72–74, 89, 90, 108, 140–142; out-of-pocket expenses, 73; professional fees, 73; selection of, 72–74. *See also* Fair Practice Code

147

G

Gardner, John W., 95, 96, 109, 139, 140
Gemmell, Edgar M., 141
Gide, André, 122
Gift opportunities, 18, 22, 43, 47–49, 53, 56, 57, 78, 111, 114
Gift tables, 83, 84, 138
Gifts by type: advance, 16, 41, 42; general, 16, 41, 42; major, 16, 41, 42; planned. *See* Planned gifts; special, 16, 17, 41, 42
Gifts, forms of: cash, 51; planned, 43, 52, 54, 87, 88; securities, 51; tangible personal property and real estate, 51, 52
Gifts of future interests, 51, 79, 115, 134, 135
Goals, 101–103, 113, 135; "stretch," 20, 46, 77. *See also* Annual giving campaigns, goals; Capital funds campaigns, goals
Government: as source of support, 45, 48; grants, 16; in philanthropy, 94, 104, 118

H

Harvard University, 87

I

Independent Sector, 109
Inflation, 13, 104, 119
Investment committee, 64

K

Kentucky, 92
Kimball, Norman H., 70

L

Legislation: The Tax Reform Act of 1969, 94, 97. *See also* Regulation of charities
Life insurance policies, 52, 79
List brokers, 91
Los Angeles Music Center, 81
Louisiana, 130

M

Mail appeal, 14, 20, 22–24, 29, 109, 117; guidelines, 68, 122–126; list brokers, 91
Maintenance (maintenance funds), 13, 104, 114
Matching challenge grants, 99, 107
Mellon Foundation, Andrew W., 98
Memberships (dues), 71, 72, 107
Motivations for giving, 34, 35, 121
Museum of Modern Art, The, 71, 81, 104, 105

N

Named gift opportunities. *See* Gift opportunities
National Audubon Society, 98

INDEX

National Committee for Responsive Philanthropy, 113
National Council on Philanthropy, 109
National Health Council, 96
National Information Bureau, 28, 96
National Society of Fund-Raising Executives, 96
National voluntary health organizations, 106, 107
Neighborhood Housing Services, 98
New York City, 31
New York Philharmonic, 132
New York Times, The, 31, 95, 139, 140
Nominating Committee, 64
Nonprofit organizations, 119
Nucleus fund, 86

O

Oklahoma, 130
Operating funds, 13, 104, 107
Organizations: as affected by inflation, 119; core groups, 12; financially conservative trend of, 118, 119; gift-supported, 11, 12; tax deductibility, 12

P

Patron, 21, 22, 47, 53, 78, 79, 134
Payroll deduction plan, 90, 91
Penn Foundation, William, 98
Philadelphia, 98
Philanthropy, (preface), 118, 120
Philanthropy Monthly, The, 92
Phonathons, 33, 34
Planned gifts, 43, 56, 57, 96, 115, 133–135. *See* Bequests, Charitable income trusts, Charitable remainder trusts, Gifts of future interests, Life insurance policies
Pledges, 39, 50, 51; acknowledgment of, 58; confirmation in writing, 57, 58; legally binding, 77; payments of, 41, 53, 105. *See* Capital funds campaign, pledges
Princeton University, 141
Private sector, the, 129, 130
Professional fund raiser, (preface), 35, 36, 101. *See also* Professional staff
Professional staff (campaign staff) (development department), 28, 30, 35–37, 44, 46, 49, 50, 68, 69, 74, 88, 89, 101
Projects, 16; bazaar, 33; journal, 33; thrift shop, 33
Promotions, 16; calendar, 33; cards for major holidays, 33; personalized stationery, 33
Prospect assignment, 49, 50
Prospect evaluation, 46
Prospect involvement, 86, 87
Prospect research, 109
Prospects (prospective donors), 101, 104, 109, 117. *See also* Annual giving campaigns, prospects; Capital funds campaigns, prospects

149

Public announcement, 21, 60, 86, 117
Public television, 107
Publicity, 31, 32, 59, 60, 117; external, 60; internal, 60; magazines, 60; press, 31; radio, 31; television, 31

R

Radiothons, 70
Receipt form, official, 26
Recognition categories. *See* Benefactor, Donor, Patron, Sponsor
Red Cross, 130
Regulation of charities, 28, 91, 92, 95, 118. *See also* Legislation
Release time, 116
Retires, 116
Roche, Robert P., 108, 141–143
Rockefeller, John D., Jr., 30, 31
Rockefeller, John D., 3rd., 108
"Rule of Thirds," 83, 84, 137

S

Schwartz, John J., 108
Seymour, Harold J., 52
Smith College, 81
Solicitation: in-person, 14, 22–24, 29, 43, 52, 111, 126; of assigned prospects, 24–26; of board members, 14, 16
Solicitors, *See* Volunteer solicitors

Solicitors' progress report, 26
Sources of support, 66; corporations, 48; foundations, 48; government, 45, 48; individuals, 48
"Specific Situation Formula," 84, 137
Sponsor, 21, 47, 53, 78, 79
Statement of intent, 57, 58
Students, 116

T

Tax benefits, 27, 43, 51, 54, 94
Tax deductibility. *See* Tax benefits
Telethons, 33, 34; when to consider, 69, 70
Texas, 130
Trends in fund raising: future, 111–120; recent, 93–110
Trust for Cultural Resources, The, 105

U

United Cerebral Palsy of New York, 70
United Negro College Fund, 22
United Way of America, 15, 16, 90, 91, 97
Universities, 12, 95, 101, 103
Urban problems, 24, 69, 129, 130

V

Visiting Committees (Harvard Uni-

INDEX

versity), 87
Volunteer committees, 45, 46; advance gifts, 16, 42; annual giving, 14–17; evaluations, 46; major gifts, 41, 42; planned giving, 43; special gifts, 16, 17, 41, 42, 49; sponsoring, 79, 80; steering, 77
Volunteer fund raisers. *See* Volunteer solicitors
Volunteer leaders, 49, 60, 63–92, 132; as signers of mail appeals, 123; availability, 99, 100; informed on fund raising, 100
Volunteers: as a way of life, 100; effectiveness of, 118; men, 116; need for, 11; number in U.S., (preface); patterns of service, 100, 116; women, 11, 116
Volunteer solicitors, 9, 11–37, 39–61, 63, 67, 68, 82, 83, 96, 103
Volunteer workers. *See* Volunteer solicitors

W

Watts (Los Angeles), 98
Wilder, Thornton, 121
WNET/Channel 13, 107

Y

Young, Whitney, Jr., 129

About the author

MAURICE G. GURIN is a member of the board of directors of the American Association of Fund-Raising Counsel and a former board member of the National Society of Fund-Raising Executives. Among the present and former clients of The Gurin Group, the fund-raising consulting firm he heads, are The Ford Foundation, The Museum of Modern Art, the New York Philharmonic, the Whitney Museum, CARE, the United Negro College Fund, United Service Organizations (USO), the Metropolitan Opera, the Fresh Air Fund, the Council on Foreign Relations, Radcliffe College, WNET/Channel 13, and other equally renowned organizations.